ASSAILING

the

GATES

of

HELL

CHRISTIANITY AT WAR
WITH THE LEFT

JAN ADRIAAN SCHLEBUSCH

REFORMATION ZION PUBLISHING

Cover art by Daniel Brannan Art
Published 2022
Printed in the United States of America

ISBN:
978-1-956521-08-5 - Paperback
978-1-956521-10-8 - ePub
978-1-956521-11-5 - Kindle

CONTENTS

FOREWORD

Christianity is a religion of conflict. This is because forces of evil exist that oppose God and His law. The devil has been recruiting fellow rebels since the garden of Eden, and his army is vast. Satan deceived the nations prior to the coming of Christ, and those nations waged war against the Old Testament people of God. However, now that Christ has been given all authority in heaven and on earth, the nations are no longer being deceived but are being discipled by Christ (Matthew 28:18-19; Revelation 20:3).

The kingdom of Christ has continued to expand since His resurrection from the dead (Matthew 13:31-32). What was once a sect of Judaism has grown to become the largest religion in the world, taking over the Roman Empire and becoming the dominant force in Europe. Of course, the church experienced setbacks with the rise of Islam. But then Christianity spread throughout the world alongside European expansion into the Americas, Africa, and beyond.

Today, the greatest threat to Christ's kingdom is the secular Leftism that arose post-Christendom. Western Christian nations have abandoned Christ in droves, and the enemies of Christ have infiltrated every major institution—courts and civil government, universities, public schools, and the media. The Left seeks to outlaw Christian morality, destroy the family unit, erase our history, and train up children as soldiers for their cause. The opposition seems overwhelming.

Yet this adversary too shall fade into oblivion, as the nations plot in vain and shall be conquered by the Lord Jesus (Psalm 2:1, 8). Why then does it feel like the church is losing today? We must remember that there are always ups and downs in the history of Christ's kingdom. But Christ is playing the long game. The Cultural Marxists made the "long march through the institutions." However, their strategy is short-term compared to the sovereign plan of Almighty God. What we are experiencing today looks bleak for the future of Christ's kingdom. But it will prove to be a blip on the radar in the grand scheme of things.

Nevertheless, it is important to emphasize that Christ will accomplish His dominion by means of His church. He works in and through His people to accomplish His purposes. So this is no time for passivity. Christians must respond properly to the attacks we face. Yet to do so, we must comprehend the current situation, and that means understanding how we got here.

And for that we have Jan Adriaan Schlebusch as our guide. Dr. Schlebusch explains the history of Liberalism and how it led to the Cultural Marxism under which we now suffer. For it is only in understanding the philosophy and strategy of our adversaries that we can form a truly effective counterstrategy. Dr. Schlebusch urges Christians to not just play defense in countering the subversive tactics of our opponents. The Left has made war with Christianity. So we must fight back. The church must go on the offensive, assailing the gates of hell that Jesus promised shall not prevail against it (Matthew 16:18).

Zachary Garris
Pastor of Bryce Avenue Presbyterian Church (PCA)
White Rock, New Mexico

INTRODUCTION

On the 8th of May 1794, in Paris, France, the Committee for Public Safety publicly executed the father
of modern chemistry. Antoine Lavoisier was one
of the greatest scientists of all time. He discovered
the role of oxygen in combustion. He was the first
person to recognize and name the chemical element
hydrogen. He was the first to recognize that water
consists of oxygen and hydrogen. He wrote the first
periodic table. But there was a problem: he was a
Christian. He believed in Jesus Christ. He believed
that the Bible, which he called "Holy Scripture,"
to be authentic and to hold authority over people.[1]
His beliefs posed a threat to public safety.

He had to die. The threat that his beliefs posed
to public safety in France was evident to the judge
with whom Lavoisier's wife pleaded for his life.
Marie-Anne, a renowned chemist herself, assisted
her husband in his work. She was only 36 years
old when her husband was sentenced to death. Her

---

1. Dave Armstrong, *Science and Christianity: Close
Partners or Mortal Enemies* (Morrisville, NC: Lulu,
2012), 278.

husband was only 50. She would not only lose her research partner, but her soulmate. Marie-Anne pleaded with the judge that her husband could, and that they could together, still contribute so much to the field of chemistry if his life was spared. But Judge Coffinhal simply responded, "The Republic needs neither scholars nor chemists; the course of justice cannot be delayed."[2] Like her husband, Marie-Anne's father, Jacques, was also a devout Christian, who had worked together with her husband in reforming the tax system and helping the poor prior to the French Revolution.[3] They both longed to see Christianity's impact upon society increase. And as a result, Marie-Anne would lose not only her husband but also her father on the same day—both decapitated by the guillotine—for the sake of the "safety" of the general public.

Liberal historians may tell you that I am failing to provide the full context of this story. After all, this was France in 1794, the height of the advent of modern liberalism, one of the most progressive and enlightened governments of all time. The liberal historian may claim Lavoisier and his father-in-law were executed because they opposed settled

2. Henri Wallon, *Histoire du Tribunal révolutionnaire de Paris avec le Journal de ses actes,* Volume 3 (Paris: Hachette, 1881), 402.

3. Kenneth Davis, *The Cautionary Scientists: Priestley, Lavoisier, and the Founding of Modern Chemistry* (New York: Putnam, 1966), 78.

science, they opposed progress, and they were trai-
tors to their government.

For the sake of comparison, remember that
in the first century following the resurrection of
Christ, Christianity was not officially outlawed
in the Roman empire. However, Rome's progressive policy of religious freedom on paper did not
prevent 11 of the 12 apostles from getting murdered because of their convictions regarding the
(socio-political) implications of the Lordship of
Jesus Christ.[4] The Persian religion of Zoroastrian-
ism, for example, was tolerated within the Roman
Empire along with Greco-Roman paganism.[5] But
because this religion did not confess nor promote any divine authority higher than that of the
Roman Emperor, it was not considered a threat like
Christianity. Like the apostles of the first century,
Lavosier was considered a threat to the social order
(or "public safety") of the time.

Lavoisier opposed the scientific establishment.
During the Age of Enlightenment of the eighteenth
century, settled science taught that fire was caused
by setting off fire-like elements called "phlogiston."
Objects that are easy to set ablaze were taught to
be high in "phlogiston." To the contrary Lavoisier,

4. W.C. Hinzie, *Secrets of the Apostles: The Stories
You Do Not Hear in Sunday School* (Bloomington, IN:
WestBow Press, 2011), 28.

5. Albert de Jong, *Traditions of the Magi: Zoroas-
trianism in Greek and Latin Literature* (Leiden: Brill,
1997), 310.

however, proposed that it is combustion, the chemical reaction between a fuel and an oxidant, which causes fire.[6]

Lavoisier opposed progress. He wanted to maintain the French monarchy and much of the old Christian social order. He criticized the liberalism of the likes of the prominent revolutionary statesman Marat and considered him unqualified to be a member of the French Academy of Sciences.[7]

Lavoisier also opposed the government. After all, he had tried his best to avoid the triumph of liberalism through the bloody French Revolution by introducing and proposing many tax and social reforms in the 1780s, all of which could potentially have killed off the very spark that ignited the new order.

Lavoisier is not unlike some modern Christians. In the midst of the coronavirus lockdowns of 2021, there was a Canadian pastor named James Coates who refused to follow government health restrictions on public gatherings. Coates, like Lavoisier more than 200 years before him, was regarded to be a threat to public safety by virtue of practicing the Christian religion—in his particular case the biblical command of Hebrews 10:25 to never "for-

6. James Bryant Conant, *The Overthrow of Phlogiston Theory: The Chemical Revolution of 1775–1789* (Cambridge: Harvard University Press, 1950), 14.

7. Harold Hartley, "Antoine Laurent Lavoisier: 26 August 1743 – 8 May 1794," *Journal of the Royal Society* 189 (June 1946): 452.

sake the assembling of ourselves together." Coates was persecuted and imprisoned for continuing to hold church services in spite of government restrictions on public gatherings.[8]

Coates opposed the scientific establishment. Not only did he conduct church services for gatherings far exceeding the number allowed by the Public Health Agency, but attendees at the services were also predominantly maskless despite the recommendations by the scientific establishment. Now, it is of course true that masking has not significantly contributed to stopping the spread of Covid-19, nor have the lockdowns been saving lives (as research published in leading medical journals have confirmed).[9] But the fact that the sci-

---

8. Ted Clarke, "Rally planned for Saturday to support jailed minister," *Prince George Citizen* (February 26 2021), https://www.princegeorgecitizen.com/news/rally-planned-for-saturday-to-support-jailed-minister-1.24287764.

9. Michael Klompas, Charles Morris, Julia Sinclair, Madelyn Pearson, and Erika Shenoy, "Universal Masking in Hospitals in the Covid-19 Era," *The New England Journal of Medicine* 63 (2020): 1-3; Eran Brendavit, Christopher Oh, Jay Bhattacharya, and John Ioannidis, "Assessing mandatory stay-at-home and business closure effects on the spread of COVID-19," *European Journal of Clinical Investigation* 51 (2020): 1-9; Quentin De Larochelambert, Andy Marc, Juliana Antero, Eric Le Bourg, and Jean-François Toussaint, "Covid-19 Mortality: A Matter of Vulnerability Among Nations Facing Limited Margins of Adaptation," *Frontiers in Public Health* 8.604339 (2020): 1-11; Christopher R. Berry, Anthony

entific community in general has mostly failed to recognize this truth meant that James Coates, like Lavoisier, found himself in direct opposition to the scientific establishment.

Coates opposed progress. After all, the idea that the church remains independent of government control is one that has long been regarded as outdated by leftist scholars. They view the centralized government control characteristic of social democracy as the ultimate fulfilment of human progress and advancement throughout history.[10]

Coates opposed the government. He, like his devout Christian predecessors, chose to obey God rather than the government, and for this reason he spent 33 days locked up in prison. Coates opposed, indeed threatened, the heart and soul of leftist politics: the all-powerful and all-interfering centralized state.

The French Revolutionary government that murdered Lavoisier and the Canadian government that imprisoned Coates, though separated by over two centuries of history, should rightly be regarded as two of the most Leftist governments in history. Both these governments claim

---

Fowler, Tamara Glazer, Samantha Handel-Meyer, and Alec MacMillen, "Evaluating the effects of shelter-in-place policies during the COVID-19 pandemic," *Proceedings of the National Academy of Sciences of the United States of America* 118(15) (2021): 1-6.

10. Francis Fukuyama, *The End of History and the Last Man* (New York: Free Press, 2006), 48.

to be Liberal, and in a sense that is true, at least in terms of the theoretical foundations of their political agendas. However, although Liberalism is not synonymous with Leftism, it did provide the philosophical foundations for political Leftism. In order to understand what drives these people and the movements they represent, we need to look at how Leftist politics historically developed from the philosophy of Liberalism.

The first chapter of this book is therefore dedicated to a historical investigation regarding the Liberal origins of the Left. However, this book is not primarily about Liberalism. Nor is it about Leftism. Rather, the focus of this book is the necessity of *countering the subversive strategies* used by Leftists to infiltrate and destroy Christianity from the inside out, with the purpose of *not only stopping but ultimately pulverizing this enemy of Christ and His church*. This is a necessity because, as followers of Jesus Christ, we are called not only to defend but to advance His kingdom (2 Corinthians 5:20; Matthew 28:18-20). In particular, this book is about the need for an active and militant resistance against the currently prevailing Leftist or Marxist agenda of systematic infiltration aimed at subverting and ultimately destroying every Christian institution and culture on the planet. But in order to even understand these strategies and tactics through which the Left seeks to destroy us, we need a clear picture of what the Left is all about in terms of its ideas, origins, and purposes, as well as by contrast what Christianity entails—hence the focus of our first chapter. The second chapter will provide a thorough overview of Marxism as a philosophical system by showing how it is ultimately aimed at usurping the authority of God. The third chapter will explain the subversive strategies employed by Cultural Marxists in particular over the past century and explain the reasons behind their success. The fourth chapter will shift to answering the question of how we ended up in the current socio-religious and socio-political predicament by showing how and where the church has miserably failed in its calling to resist the Marxist onslaught. Finally, the fifth chapter will conclude the book by taking a practical look at how we are to go about fulfilling our call and duty as the Church Militant in the battle against the forces of darkness in our contemporary context.

CHAPTER 1

Liberalism: The History of an Idea

TERMS LIKE "LIBERAL" and "conservative" or "left" and "right" are often used loosely in public discourse and media, often with neither the author nor the audience knowing what they mean. In the United States, Republican voters often identify as conservative, while Democratic voters usually identify as liberal. Opinion polls are regularly conducted wherein the general public can identify themselves as either "conservative," "moderate," or "liberal." However, it is doubtful that the general public, as a rule, actually knows what these terms entail. And contrary to what your local postmodern deconstructionist college professor may claim, words simply cannot mean whatever you want them to mean. If they could, all communication between humans would become completely impossible.

In order to understand what Liberalism really means, we need to take a look at the historical development of the idea of Liberalism. The central idea behind Liberalism is as old as mankind itself. What the snake promised Eve as reward for her disobedience to God's command, was the ability to "be like God, knowing good and evil." (Genesis 3:5). The Hebrew word commonly translated as "knowing," עָדַ, also entails the notion of "determining" or "deciding." In other words, what the snake essentially promised Eve was the ability to become her own god, her own authority, and her own lawgiver. This desire for divinization, for absolute sovereignty and the rebellion against the sovereignty of God it entails, lies at the very heart of Liberalism.

The same idea was, of course, also prevalent in ancient paganism. The pre-Socratic philosopher Protagoras (490—420 B.C.), for example, famously articulated what would become known as the "homo mensura" principle: the idea that mankind itself, as the measure and standard of all things ("ἄνθρωπος μέτρον"), has the right to determine good and evil.[1] As a socio-political phenomenon, what we have come to know as Modern Liberalism, however, was a much later development out of similar ideas associated with a philosophical movement in Europe in the seventeenth and eighteenth centuries called the Enlightenment. The ideas behind this movement would finally manifest in society with the famous French Revolution at

1. Michael Nill, *Morality and Self-Interest in Protagoras, Antiphon, and Democritus* (Leiden: Brill, 1985), 4.

the end of the eighteenth century. The ideas of the Enlightenment have, to a large degree, shaped the world we currently live in. The Enlightenment also gave us the concepts of "Right" and "Left," as well as "Conservative" and "Liberal." But what was the Enlightenment exactly?

The Enlightenment

The word "enlightenment" assumes the existence of darkness. As a historical phenomenon, the Enlightenment supposedly brought civilization from darkness to light. But this immediately raises the question—what exactly constitutes darkness and what constitutes light? The Bible clearly teaches that Jesus Christ is the Light of the world and that outside of his presence and will, people remain in darkness (John 8:12). In other words, the enlightenment of the human mind and heart cannot take place outside of Christ. A true enlightenment will therefore bring us from the darkness of sin, Satan, and death into the light and love of Jesus Christ. But is this what the Enlightenment in Europe in the seventeenth and eighteenth centuries accomplished? The answer is a resounding and emphatic no!

In fact, the Enlightenment was a reaction against Christendom, that is, against the old European social and political order based on Christian principles. One of the first Enlightenment thinkers was a French philosopher by the name René

Descartes, who lived between the years 1596 and 1650. The reader might be familiar with his most famous claim, "I think, therefore I am" (*cogito ergo sum* in the original Latin). But what did Descartes mean by this? Descartes believed that because our senses can deceive us, the only source of undoubted knowledge must lie within our mind. Having then excluded all that is observable and what he considered to be doubtable from the equation, he concluded that the only firm foundation for sure, indubitable knowledge is human reason alone. For Descartes, reason served as the last bastion against all doubt. While all that was external of the human mind might be potentially deceptive, the internal cognitive consciousness of one's own thinking served as the irrefutable proof of one's own existence.[2]

There are a number of philosophical problems with Descartes' rationalist theory. When we are asleep and we dream, for example, we perceive something that is neither real nor true, but this deception is wholly within our own mind and occurs without the use of sensual perception. In other words, the mind can deceive us just as easily as our senses can. Secondly, Descartes' belief in the human mind or "pure reason" as existing independently of all "external" realities is illogical and unrealistic. For example, the mind itself, if strictly

---

2. Rene Descartes, *Principia Philsophiae* (Amsterdam: Elzevier, 1644), 30.

separated from everything else, cannot tell you whether the thoughts it is thinking are your own or someone else's. Cartesian rationalism wrongly ascribes to the human mind an independence and ability to acquire unmediated knowledge that man, as dependent and created being, could never achieve. The existence of any self-consciousness on the part of man already presupposes a consciousness of that which is not the self, which negates the possibility of any unmediated or autonomous knowledge. In other words, since man is a created being, any self-consciousness on the part of man can only come into existence within a created framework provided and revealed by God as Creator and ultimate First Cause. For this reason Christ, as Logos, is the Source and Foundation of logic and reasoning. Moreover, Christianity has always maintained a sharp distinction between created and uncreated or dependent and independent being. Maintaining this distinction is also central to an orthodox Christology, as the two natures of Christ are unconfused and unmixed. As the Westminster Confession of Faith teaches in chapter 8, paragraph 2: "[In Christ] the two whole, perfect, and distinct natures, the Godhead and the manhood, were inseparably joined together in one person, without conversion, composition, or confusion."

"I think, therefore I am" is the false conclusion of a false philosophy. But it is the philosophy upon which the Enlightenment was built. It is a philosophy that strove to liberate the individual human from everything that binds him to anything outside of himself. It is man's attempt at being his own god and replacing the Triune God as the Source of all truth (Proverbs 1:7; Isaiah 48:17) with man himself. As long as God is acknowledged as our Creator, we are necessarily bound to His design and purpose for our lives—that is, bound to His sovereignty over us. The Enlightenment would have none of this.

Questions such as "where does authority come from?" or "why does someone or something have authority over someone or something else?" are questions which have preoccupied philosophers for millennia. The Enlightenment's answer was that there is no higher authority than the individual. The individual is god. In developing their theory of society (or social ontology), the Enlightenment used this same idea of human independence and sovereignty as its foundational point of departure. Philosophers associated with the Enlightenment such as Thomas Hobbes (1588–1679), John Locke (1632–1704), and Jean-Jacques Rousseau (1712–1788) based their social and political theory on the idea known as the "social contract." The central assumption of social contract theory is that every individual human being is sovereign and independent of both God and the reality that God has created. Since every individual human being is by nature completely independent, the idea of the social contract proposed that these individual human beings, unknowingly and unconsciously, enter into an agreement with each other to establish a society and a socio-political order in which some exercise authority over others.[3]

Consequently, for the likes of Rousseau, there exists no natural authority in society. Everyone is equal. Parents have no authority over their children, for example. God has no authority over humanity either. Because there is no created structure to society, human society is brought about by this implicit agreement between sovereign individuals rather than by the will of God. Every man, woman, and child are their own god.

But of course, this is a radical distortion of reality. A baby, prior to being born, does not choose his own mother nor the family and nation he will be born into. None of us chooses the place or time of our birth, nor do we even choose our own names. These are simply realities over which we have no control. The idea that we "implicitly agreed" to any of this is utterly absurd. And it is absurd because it is based on the absurd idea of human sovereignty. It is rooted in the same rebellion against the sovereignty and truthfulness of God that informed the snake's lie in the Garden of Eden: "You will not surely die" (Genesis 3:4).

Surprisingly, there are still many Christians

---

3. Jean Jacques Rousseau, *Du contrat social, ou, Principes du droit politique* (Amsterdam: M.M. Rey, 1762), 68-70.

who fail to understand this. Even contemporary Christian scholars, such as Kevin DeYoung, Council member of the Gospel Coalition and associate professor of systematic theology at Reformed Theological Seminary in Charlotte, North Carolina, argues that opposition to the Enlightenment on the part of Christians amounts to a "pseudo-intellectual explanation of what they don't like" and that we should not "misread the Enlightenment as everywhere... anti-Christian."[4] But DeYoung oversimplifies the matter and seems to confuse a distinct philosophical movement with a historical time period. There was undoubtedly a definitive overarching theme in Enlightenment thought which effectuated (albeit in some cases perhaps only implicitly and subconsciously) an epistemic shift[5] away from the belief in the authority of divine revelation to anthropocentrism. There were countless philosophies and ideas among the champions of the Enlightenment, but the overarching anti-Christian tendency was undoubtedly there. There were certainly intellectuals and philosophers who, while engaging with and opposing these false ideas, also

4. Kevin DeYoung, "Three Myths about the Enlightenment," *The Gospel Coalition* (October 16, 2018), https://www.thegospelcoalition.org/blogs/kevin-deyoung/three-myths-enlightenment/.

5. Epistemology is that branch of philosophy which deals with the nature, validity, and scope of true knowledge, and how it is to be distinguished from false knowledge.

borrowed concepts and vocabulary from the liberal Enlightenment thinkers, but these historical figures should still be regarded as Counter-Enlightenment thinkers, even if in some cases only eclectically so. A central problem with DeYoung's argument is that he concedes to a historical narrative which wrongly equates the Enlightenment with progress—a fallacy I will expose later in this chapter. The Presbyterian philosopher Rousas John Rushdoony (1916–2001) explains how Enlightenment thought sought to supplant the traditional Christian social order:

> The Enlightenment shifted the center of interest from God to man, and from the Church to the State... Man was now the measure of all things, and it was man's will that needed to be done... Enlightenment humanism began with the 'moral baggage' of its context, Christendom, but, in practice, it steadily stripped off all morality in favor of self-enjoyment. At the same time, being at war with God, profanation became a prized pleasure... One of the quiet goals of the Enlightenment was the disestablishment of Churches and of Christianity... A first step in this process of disestablishment was to reduce Christianity to an option for man, a matter of choice, not of necessity. The realm of necessity was held to be the civil government. Freedom came to mean deliverance from the Church to the State,

from supernatural mandates and laws to 'natural' and statist laws. The Reformation had said plainly that Biblical faith requires belief in God's predestination, in God's sovereign choice... This was reversed by the Enlightenment, and then by Arminianism. Sovereign choice was transferred to man. Man, it was held, has the option to choose God or reject Him, to declare God to be elect or non-elect.[6]

Heresies ascribing sovereignty to mankind have also been rejected by faithful Christians throughout the history of the church. The church father Augustine (354—450), for example, refuted rationalism when he wrote that since "reason (*rationalis*) itself is depraved, as it had been previously in me, it remains ignorant and must be enlightened by another light so that it may be a partaker of truth, seeing that of itself it cannot understand the nature of truth."[7] For Augustine, therefore, the light of divine revelation needs to sanctify reason before

6. Rousas John Rushdoony, *To Be as God: A Study of Modern Thought since the Marquis de Sade* (Vallecito, CA: Ross House, 2003), 9-10, 17.

7. Aurelius Augustine, *Confessiones* (London: Revington, 2010 [400]), IV, 25. This is my own translation of the original Latin, which reads "rationalis mens ipsa vitiosa est, qualis in me tunc erat, nesciente alio lumine illam inlustrandam esse, ut sit particeps veritatis, quia non est ipsa natura veritatis, quoniam tu inluminabis lucernam meam."

it can acquire true knowledge. At the start of the twelfth century, a scholastic philosopher named Peter Abelard (1079—1142) also advocated for a rationalist philosophy that made man himself the epistemological center and starting point, that is, the foundation and standard of knowledge and truth. Because of this, Abelard is widely considered to be one of the great forebears of modern Liberalism.[8] During his own time, however, he was brilliantly opposed by the great French monk, Bernard of Clairvaux (1090—1153), who emphasized that faith in God is the highest form of knowledge, as this knowledge directly comes to us from the omnipotent King of the universe.[9]

Like Augustine and Bernard, many Christians during Descartes' own lifetime refuted his rationalism. The Dutch Reformed theologian and philosopher Gisbertus Voetius (1589–1676), for example, brilliantly showed how faith as a gift from the Creator and Lawgiver of the universe trumps depraved reason inasmuch as the latter remains ignorant of many great truths for as long as it remains unenlightened by divine revelation itself.[10]

In reality, the Enlightenment provided a false

---

8. William Gerber, *American Liberalism: Laudable End, Controversial Means* (Detroit: Twayne, 1975), 129.

9. Bernard Clairvoux, *Opera, epistolae ad Innocent II* (n.d), 1442.

10. Gisbertus Voetius, *Ratio Humana in rebus fidei* (Amsterdam: Wormser, 1636), 4.

enlightenment. It is not worthy of the name. True enlightenment entails being drawn closer to the Lord of the universe, Jesus Christ. The movement known as the Enlightenment in reality did the opposite. Its benefits to humanity have also been overemphasized by liberal historians. It is certainly true that the Industrial Revolution, which chronologically followed the Enlightenment, brought about many advances and laid the foundations of modern industry and technology. However, the Enlightenment itself is wrongly credited with the fact that we live more comfortably in the twenty-first century than in centuries prior.

There are a number of historical problems with this theory, as it is based on the fallacy that historical correlation equals causation, widely known in historiography as the *post hoc ergo propter hoc* fallacy ("after this, therefore because of this"). First, this theory disregards the fact that it was not the men of the Enlightenment but rather the church monasteries, particularly in England in the sixteenth century, that should be credited with the greatest contributions to laying the foundations for the invention of cast iron, the key ingredient that ushered in the Industrial Revolution.[11]

Secondly, it is unlikely that the technological advances of modernity are completely without any kind of historical precedent. Shortly after Adam

11. Thomas Woods, *How the Catholic Church Built Western Civilization* (Washington, DC: Regnery, 2005), 37.

and Eve's fall, in the world prior to the flood, people lived about ten times longer than they do today. While there are certainly geological factors which caused this, it is interesting to note that in the pre-flood history, there is no record of any human being dying in infancy. Furthermore, of Noah's 9 progenitors from Adam to Lamech, only one (Lamech, who also lived to see the age of 777—see Genesis 5:31) died prior to reaching a lifespan of nine centuries, which means that both their nutrition (and by extension their agricultural practices), as well as their medical practices, had to be highly advanced. Although Moses, the author of Genesis would have been ignorant of cast iron and machine tools, the biblical text still hints that these may have already been invented prior to the flood (Genesis 4:22), implying that some of the great technological advances made prior to the flood may have been obliterated because the scientific writings of the time were not preserved on the ark. That the flood not merely ended the lives of the godless on the earth during Noah's day, but obliterated the civilizational advances of the time, is hinted at by the Apostle Peter when he writes that the very "world that then existed [i.e. prior to the flood] perished" (2 Peter 3:6). It is false assumption that the secular humanism associated the Enlightenment is in any way a logical or historical precursor to great technological and industrial advancement. In fact, the most notable contributions to technological advancement have actually been made over two centuries after the Enlightenment and often in those societies where the spirit of the Enlightenment has been most evidently rejected. In many regards, the immense technological advancement of the past few decades should be regarded as a liberation from the limitations imposed on mankind by the Enlightenment's epistemic elevation of the mind and the senses. As Rushdoony points out:

> Technology has been made an inescapable part of cultural activity and added a new dimension to man by liberating him from the limitations of his hands and immediate mental or physical activity. By instruments of computation and automation, man has become more fully man and added to his reach in every respect, added dimension to his life and living... To despise technology and its contributions is to despise life and time.[12]

In spite of the falsehoods and destructive theories the Enlightenment produced, its heretical ideas continued to inform much of European philosophy throughout the eighteenth century and ended up providing the basis of Liberalism and Leftist politics, which was originally manifested in the French Revolution, a socio-political upheaval that would change the character of Western civilization itself.

---

12. Rousas John Rushdoony, *Intellectual Schizophrenia: Culture, Crisis and Education* (Vallecito, CA: Ross House, 1961), 111-112.

The French Revolution

The French Revolution was the first political manifestation of the ideas of the Enlightenment. The Dutch Reformed political philosopher, Guillaume Groen van Prinsterer (1801–1876), described the ideas of "liberty, equality and fraternity" that informed the French Revolution as doctrines "derived from false speculation, which are opposed to the essence of things and therefore opposed to history, to the historic development of humanity, against all societal rights and relationships, as a fatal seed of confusion and dissolution."[13] The Southern Presbyterian pastor and philosopher Robert Lewis Dabney (1820–1898) described the French Revolution's conception of liberty as "license to trample on other people as they choose," its equality as "similar license for the Outs when they could become the Ins," and its fraternity as "all brother rogues [which lead to] all the worst oppressions and outrages."[14]

---

13. Guillaume Groen van Prinsterer, *Grondwetherziening en eensgezindheid* (Amsterdam: Johannes Müller, 1849), 483. This is my own translation from the original Dutch, which reads: "aan valsche bespiegeling ontleend, tegen het wezen der dingen en dus tegen de Geschiedenis, tegen de historische ontwikkeling der menschheid, tegen elken gegeven toestand der maatschappelijke regten en betrekkingen, als een noodlottige kiem van verwarring en ontbinding, gekant is."

14. Robert Lewis Dabney, *Discussions, Volume III: Philosophical* (Harrisonburg, VA: Sprinkle, 1892), 313.

An example of this outrageous oppression was of course the murder of Antoine Lavoisier. But the French Revolutionaries were not content with just killing Christians. They wanted to eradicate and exterminate all traces of Christianity from the face of the earth. They wanted to "liberate" themselves from God completely. They tried almost everything to accomplish this—so much so that the great South African theologian, Dr. Francis Nigel Lee (1934–2011), described the French Revolution as "the birth of the antichrist."[15]

The Revolution in France of 1789 was a radical overthrow of the existing socio-political order in France. France was a monarchy with an established royal house, as well as a strong aristocratic class. The political order was greatly decentralized, however, with local landlords, bishops, and princes all exercising political authority within their local territories. The church played a central role in society in advising and checking the actions of princes and kings, as well as being responsible for the care of the poor. The schools and universities were also administered by the church. In this way society was arranged according to the principles of the Christian religion and the culture in France, and in fact that of all of Europe was shaped by Christianity. The state of the church ebbed and flowed,

---

15. Francis Nigel Lee, *French Revolution*, audio, https://www.sermonaudio.com/saplayer/playpopup. asp?SID=21081143182.

of course, and sadly, by the late eighteenth-century the church in France was plagued by corruption and indifference. The country itself also suffered from an economic recession.[16] These circumstances made the French people more open to the false ideas and promises of Liberalism, which had at that time already been propagated in France for well over a century, yet without much success. The French philosophers, in opportunistic fashion, made use of the socio-political decline of the time to indoctrinate the French people with their false ideas.

Yet the socio-economic decline in France in the eighteenth century should not be overstated. King Louis XIV, as well as the aristocracy at the time, were not oblivious to the problems and had in fact begun working on socio-political reforms which had real potential to solve many of the societal problems in France at the time. As the historian of the French Revolution, Nesta Webster, has noted, "The work of the revolutionaries was not, however, to accelerate reforms, but to arrest them in order to increase popular discontent and bring themselves into power."[17]

It was, therefore, ultimately the relentless pro-

---

16. Edmund Burke, *Reflections on the Revolution in France, and on the Proceedings in Certain Societies in London Relative to that Event* (London: Dodsley, 1790), 213.

17. Nesta Webster, *World Revolution: The Plot against Civilization* (Boston: Small, Maynard and Company, 1921), 30.

paganda of these false ideas of the Enlightenment, rather than the socio-economic circumstances themselves, that eventually led to the French Revolution in 1789. The hatred of Christ that drove the revolutionaries is evident not only by their slaughter of Christians, but in particular by their desire to completely liberate themselves from the Lordship of Christ in every way imaginable, which manifested in some of the most godless and ludicrous political "reforms" they implemented:

1. They proclaimed a new, de-Christianized and secular republic based on the ideas of liberty, equality and fraternity.
2. This secular republic, however, had a new state religion. Christianity was replaced with the "cult of reason," the worship of the Triune God was replaced by the worship of the "goddess of reason," and churches were replaced with "Temples of Reason."
3. Even the calendar had to be de-Christianized. Because the seven-day week was too much of a reminder of God's creation of time (Exodus 20:11), it had to be abolished in favor of a 10-day week. Because the year count reminded them of the nativity of Christ, they also introduced a new, revolutionized calendar, which would be used in France for 12 years, from 1793 to 1805. The calendar consisted of 12 months of 30 days or three 10-day weeks each. In

order to make up 365 days, five holidays were simply added at the end of the year. The Sabbath and all Christian holidays like Christmas were abolished and replaced with godless feasts such as the "Festival of Reason."[18]

4. Because the Christian ideas of the family and monogamy were regarded as one of the ways in which religion had constrained the autonomy of the free individual, sexual promiscuity was promoted among the youth, in particular by means of the legalization and systematic distribution of the liberal writer Marquis de Sade's erotic and pornographic works—works which were actually widely regarded as vital to the cause of the French Revolution itself.[19]

5. The state was centralized and the new National Assembly suddenly had more political power than the French king ever dreamt of having.[20]

At the heart of the French Revolution was a hatred of Christianity. All the policies of the rev-

18. Christopher Dawson, *The Dividing of Christendom* (New York: Sheed & Ward, 1965), 225.

19. Constantin Negoita, *Implications* (New York: Hunter College, 1994), 24.

20. Guillaume Groen van Prinsterer, *Ongeloof en Revolutie* (Barneveld: Nederlands Dagblad, 1847 [revised 2008]), 227.

olutionary government had one overarching goal: abolishing Christianity and "liberating" the people from the authority of God. The French monarchy which it overthrew was hated by the liberal revolutionaries precisely because they regarded it as a representation of Christianity. The satanic spirit and the destructive effects of the French Revolution are perhaps nowhere more concisely and spectacularly described than by the father of conservatism, Edmund Burke, when he discussed the revolutionaries' treatment of the French queen Marie-Antoinette, herself a devout Christian whom they would also execute:

It is now sixteen or seventeen years since I saw the Queen of France, then the dauphiness, at Versailles; and surely never lighted this orb, which she hardly seemed to touch, a more delightful vision. I saw her just above the horizon, decorating and cheering the elevated sphere she just began to move in, glittering like the morning-star, full of life and splendour and joy. Oh, what a revolution! And what a heart I must have, to contemplate without emotion that elevation and that fall! Little did I dream when she added titles of veneration to those of enthusiastic, distant, respectful love, that she should ever be obliged to carry the sharp antidote against disgrace concealed in that bosom; little did I dream that I should have lived to see such disasters fallen upon her in a nation of gallant men, in a nation of men of honour, and of cavaliers. I thought ten thousand swords must have leaped from their scabbards to avenge even a look that threatened her with insult. But age of chivalry is gone. That of sophisters, economists and calculators has succeeded – and the glory of Europe is extinguished forever.[21]

By promoting sexual immorality through pornography in particular, the revolutionaries sought to destabilize and abolish the Christian social order. In Christianity, the family has always been regarded as the foundational unit and building block of society. Sexual intercourse serves as the consummation of the holy union between a man and a woman and is by God's design inseparable from pregnancy and children. However, by promoting sex purely as a means of pleasure, the revolutionaries individualized society by destroying the family. This promotion of sexual licentiousness was inevitably tied to their theory of society as the aggregate of free and sovereign individuals, independent of God and His created order.

All this was of course made possible by the policies sanctioned by the liberal doctrines of "liberty, equality, and fraternity." It has a nice ring to it, does it not? After all, who in his right mind would ever

---

21. Burke, *Reflections,* 89.

be opposed to freedom, fairness, or brotherhood? But these concepts, within the liberal framework which they were conceived of, represent some of the most satanic ideas ever held among men.

The liberty of liberalism is not true liberty, but a false "liberty" from all that is good, pure, and godly. It is, in reality, slavery to Satan. The practical consequences of liberalism's "liberty" is evident for all to see. In liberating the individual from the natural, loving bonds of the family, the clan, and the nation, it effectuated a universal slavery to the murderous and all-powerful state. This is the inescapable consequence of this false liberty. Think of how this tragically manifested in the legalization of abortion for example, in the twentieth century. The idea behind the right to an abortion is to liberate women from patriarchy, that is, from the authority of their fathers and husbands. If pregnancy is not a consequence of sex for men, then equality demands that it also not be a consequence for women. The individual woman is to be sexually liberated because she is her own sovereign, her own god. But what was the result? Millions upon millions of dead babies—more than half of which were probably women themselves. Moreover, this so-called sexual liberation has left women, especially those who murdered their own children through abortion, more depressed and unhappy than they have ever been, with suicide rates among young women in developed countries skyrocketing over the past few decades.[22] Liberty from God is slavery to Satan, sin, and death. There is simply no way around this.

Egalitarianism, or the doctrine of equality, disregards and spits in the face of God, Who is the Giver of all blessings (James 1:17). It is an attempt to ignore the covenantal implications of Deuteronomy 28, namely that God blesses those who obey his commands and curses those who disregard his law. Egalitarianism not only undermines God's covenant, but also his design of the social order. Authority and submission are both inescapable as no one exists in a vacuum. God designed humanity to function within a framework of authority and submission—a framework which has always been and always will remain inescapable. This is perhaps most clearly evidenced in the phenomenon of the family—the basic unit of society.

Even though the logical consequences of the liberal ideas of equality and liberty entails that parents have no real authority over their children, there are very few people on the planet who would ever deny this reality taught by natural revelation and biblical texts such as Ephesians 6:1. Likewise, husbands' authority over their wives are disregarded, to the detriment of both. Ever since the rise

---

22. Nina Stefanac, Sarah Hetrick, Carol Hulbert, Matthew J. Spittal, Katrina Witt and Jo Robinson, "Are young female suicides increasing? A comparison of sex-specific rates and characteristics of youth suicides in Australia over 2004–2014," *BMC Public Health* 19:1389 (2019), https://doi.org/10.1186/s12889-019-7742-9.

of feminism, broken marriages have almost become the norm. By virtue of no-fault divorce laws and the legalization of sodomite "marriages," millions of children have been denied one of the most basic rights guaranteed by biblical Law: the right to growing up with and prospering under the loving guidance of both a father and a mother (Exodus 20:12; Leviticus 19:3).

The Liberal doctrine of "Brotherhood" is the third devilish foundation of this philosophy. While it is true that all of humanity was made from one blood (Acts 17:26), the concept of brotherhood in itself signifies a much deeper relationship in Scripture. The Bible speaks of brotherhood as a close and special bond—either spiritual (1 Thessalonians 4:9-10), physical (Romans 9:3), or both (Philemon verse 16)—whereas Liberalism's universalization of brotherhood robs the concept of any meaning and significance. Everyone is my brother, and no one is not my brother. This idea was rooted in the very hatred of the covenantal structures of the family, the church, and the nation that characterized the Enlightenment. It separated individuals from the beauty and protection of the loving bonds that God has designed for us for our protection and to enable us to flourish, and it has left millions of people in the Western world atomized, isolated, and depressed.

Thomas Paine (1737–1809), the American liberal philosopher, acknowledged that the purpose of the French Revolution was not merely political, but fundamentally religious in nature. He wrote that the Enlightenment-based revolution in the system of government, as it manifested in France and would later manifest all over the Western world, was intrinsically connected to "a revolution in the system of religion," arguing that any connection between religion and politics is an "adulterous" one. In fact, Paine went as far as to argue that the political revolution would never be complete if not followed by this revolution in the system of religion.[23] In other words, its aim was the abolishment of Christendom as public religion in the first place, and eventually Christianity as a whole through the advocacy of apostacy from God's Law and authority. The Enlightenment had always been, at heart, an epistemological rebellion against the authority of God.

The political notions of the Left and the Right, or left-wing and right-wing, have their origins in the French Revolution and specifically in this hatred of Christianity that shaped the worldview of the French revolutionaries and, in contradistinction, the Christian resistance to it. The Bible often speaks of God's right hand as the means of provision, deliverance, and salvation (Psalms 17:7; Isaiah 41:10). Christ also rules from his position at the right hand of the Father (Acts 7:55-56; Romans 8:34; Ephesians 1:20; Colossians 3:1; Hebrews 1:3, 8:1; 10:12). Scripture even uses the image of

---

23. Thomas Paine, *The Writings of Thomas Paine* (Putnam: New York, 1896), 22.

moving to the right as walking in the ways of the Lord and moving to the left as a form of rebellion and disobedience to God (Ecclesiastes 10:2). This imagery was, after nearly 1500 years of Christianity in France, not only well-known, but also informed French culture and language. Therefore, when the French Revolution's first National Assembly was formed, supporters of the radical revolution and the overthrow of the monarchy chose to sit to the left of the chamber's president to indicate their opposition to the monarchy and the old order, while the king's supporters sat to the chamber president's right.[24] The symbolism behind this historical move was clear. The revolutionaries' identification with the Left was rooted in their liberal rebellion against all authority and the social order as ordained by a sovereign God Whom they simply refused to recognize.

Of course, because of their sheer impartibility and the devastating consequences of the aforementioned political reforms of the French Revolution, most of these revolutionary political policies would be abolished during the rise of Napoleon's dictatorship in France. Nonetheless, in the nineteenth-century, the first genuinely Leftist political theory, Marxism, evolved from the same foundations laid by the very Liberalism which inspired the French Revolution.

---

24. Robert Paxton, *Europe in the Twentieth Century* (Cengage: Boston, 1985), 214.

CHAPTER 2

Marxism: The Revolution Against Revelation

IRONICALLY, THE INDIVIDUALISM of Liberalism directly contributed to the development of the collectivist ideology in the nineteenth century called Marxism, named after its founder, the German philosopher Karl Marx (1818–1883). This may seem strange at first, and in order to understand how this historical development played out, we need to understand how the Liberalism of the French Revolution disturbed the natural social order created and ordained by God.

God, as the sovereign creator of the universe, in his wisdom, knew that it would not be good for any man to be alone (Genesis 2:18). This is why *God* created society—not man, but God. In His created order, he ordained various social structures to protect each individual human being and help him flourish. The most basic of these structures is the nuclear family. When we are born as babies, we are supposed to be born into a home with a mother and a father to nurture and care for us.

There are, of course, exceptional circumstances which can disturb this natural order of things and which are beyond our control, like the death of a parent. But thankfully the nuclear family is not the only social and covenantal structure ordained by God. The extended family is there to help care for us, as is the community in which we live. We are all part of a specific ethnic group, in which God providentially placed us in order that we may be prioritized by some when we need help and so that we can prioritize others when they are in need (1 Timothy 5:8). The church, of course, is another institution that, apart from its functions in preaching the gospel and administering the sacraments, has an obligation to see to the spiritual and physical wellbeing of its members (Galatians 6:10). All of these—the nuclear family, the clan (or extended family), the community, the nation (or *ethnos*), and the church—are social realities and covenantal structures ordained by God to not only protect us as individuals, but also to help us and those around us flourish to the glory of God.

But what the French Revolution did was attempt to destroy or at least neutralize all of these social structures. Why? Because Liberalism views them as impediments to individual sovereignty and freedom. By neutralizing these social structures, we are isolated and left vulnerable. Yes, the Liberal Revolution left the European man, as individual, vulnerable and isolated. In practice, what the social contract effectuated was to leave only one social institution remaining to usurp all the natural social functions of all others—the state. While this development took place in Europe, perhaps no one on the continent saw this more clearly than Groen van Prinsterer in the Netherlands. He wrote that Liberalism's social contract, which entailed that a free and equal aggregate of individuals unite themselves in a state, naturally implies that that state is not only the lawgiver, but also the owner of that over which it rules. Marxists then came to see that the French Revolutionary ideal of equality meant nothing as long as property rights remained intact. And in order to combat this inequality, all trade and industry had to be run by the state as the representative of the people.[1] That an all-powerful centralized state would inevitably result from Liberalism was also clearly seen from across the Atlantic by Robert Lewis Dabney, who wrote that through the social contract civil society itself becomes "a grand robber of my natural rights, which I only tolerate to save myself from more numerous robbers."[2] In the name of equality, our God-given rights to property (Exodus 20:15) and the enjoyment of the fruits of our labor (Ecclesias-

1. Guillaume Groen van Prinsterer, *Vrijheid, Gelijkheid, Broederschap: Toelichting van de spreuk der Revolutie* (The Hague: Roering, 1848), 43-44.

2. Dabney, *Discussions: Volume III*, 308.

tes 5:18-19) are thereby defrauded of any and all foundations and guarantees once the authority of God over creation and society is denied in favor of that of man. This development had in fact always been central to the chief aims of the leading orders that had promoted the French Revolution during the 1780s, such as the Continental Freemasons and the Bavarian Illuminati, as they dedicated themselves specifically to the abolition of the French Monarchy and generally to the abolition of the family, inheritance, private property, and national identity along with religion.[3]

And thus, from the ashes of the failed experiments of liberalism in France and elsewhere in Europe, Marxism arose—as was planned by the engineers of the Enlightenment from the very outset. Libertarians, who claim to be the heirs of classical Liberalism can rant against Marxism all they want. The fact of the matter is that the same ideology of liberalism with its central doctrine of egalitarianism provided the foundations of both systems. But Marxism is the heir of Liberalism not only in a philosophical, but in a very concretely historical sense. Whereas Enlightenment Liberalism sought to promote egalitarianism by targeting the aristocracy, Marxism positioned itself against what its proponents called the bourgeoisie: the newly established class of capitalists who were essentially, at least as the Marxists claimed, the

---

3. Webster, *World Revolution*, 22-23.

beneficiaries of the democratization brought about by the Enlightenment.[4]

Marxism is fundamentally based on the philosophy of materialism. While Marxism is most well-known for its economic theory of socialism, in which the state repossesses (or rather steals) all property and the means of production,[5] this economic theory is fundamentally based on their materialist worldview. This has been aptly described by Dr. Francis Nigel Lee:

> When [the Marxist philosopher] Engels remarks that 'the materialist world outlook is simply the concept of nature as it is, we must immediately ask him: 'But how is nature?' When Marxists deny the very possibility of the existence of a 'Supreme Being shut out from the whole existing world' it is clear that they regard all being as confined to the existing world or cosmos (i.e., to the whole existing material universe and not only our earth), and that they also regard each part of the Universe as on the same level of being with all the other parts by denying any part of being a 'supreme' position over against others. And with this

---

4. Max Horkheimer & Theodor Adorno, *Dialectic of Enlightenment*, trans. Edmund Jephcott (Stanford, CA: Stanford University Press, 2001), 69-71.

5. Karl Marx, *Das Kapital: Buch I* (1867; repr., Washington DC: Regnery, 2012), 336.

denial of the Supreme Being Marxists necessarily proclaim the independence of what from the Christian viewpoint is only dependent created being, thus absolutizing the relative and deifying the universe, and thus distorting the relation of the cosmos' unity to diversity.[6]

This philosophical Materialism which presupposes atheism shapes the Marxist worldview, and is manifested not only in its economic theory, but also in its philosophy of science, its historiography, and its understanding of human society. For Marx and Engels, scientific knowledge is man-made, not God-given. Science is not so much about discovering truths as created beings dependent upon God, but about creating and implementing those truths ourselves. As such, they ridicule the very philosophical quest for true knowledge in favor of a theoretical framework for how man can remake the world in its own image.[7] This dynamic is brilliantly (and prophetically) elucidated by the Dutch Neo-Calvinist theologian Herman Bavinck (1854—1921):

> In abandoning an absolute standard for judging good and evil, scholars attempt to

6. Francis Nigel Lee, *Communism Versus Creation* (Nutley, NJ: Craig Press, 1969), 35-36.

7. Karl Marx and Friedrich Engels, *Die Duitsche Ideologie* (1846; repr. Berlin: Karl-Maria Guth, 2016), 5.

utilize statistics and history to evaluate what would in the future be regarded as normative in terms of truth, law and ethics. "The greatest happiness for the greatest number" becomes the sole norm in religion, morality, logic, and aesthetics. In itself, everything is a private matter—a matter of taste and passion or of character and education. But because this would lead to licentious arbitrariness, individualism needs to be subdued by socialism. Science, represented by an areopagus of scholars, must therefore prescribe to everyone, on the basis of their own historical and statistical analysis, what constitutes truth. They constitute the highest authority.[8]

---

8. Herman Bavinck, *Christelijke Wetenschap* (Kampen: Kok, 1904), 68. This is my own translation from the original Dutch which reads: "Omdat zij echter den absoluten maatstaf tot beoordeeling van goed en kwaad hebben prijsgegeven, trachten zij aan historie en statistiek de gegevens te ontleenen, die bepalen, wat in de toekomst voor waarheid, recht, zedelijkheid enz. gehouden moet worden. The greatest happiness of the greatest number wordt de norma voor religie en moraal, voor logica en aesthetica. Op zichzelf beschouwd, is alles Privatsache, een quaestie van aanleg en smaak, van karakter en opvoeding. Maar wijl dit beginsel tot bandelooze willekeur zou leiden, moet het individualisme door het socialisme beteugeld worden. De wetenschap, vertegenwoordigd in een areopagus van geleerden, moet dus voor ieder uitmaken en vaststellen, wat op grond van historische en statistische gegevens als waarheid en recht te gelden heeft. Zij heeft het hoogste gezag."

When a Marxist does history, there is no room for the role of providence or even for the role of principles or ideas in shaping the history of the world. Everything is reduced to a material or economic struggle between the classes. Likewise, all of society is cast as being continually involved in this struggle. There can be no room for the role of the family, of nations or of religion in shaping history. All of these so-called phenomena are seen as distorted manifestations of the economic struggle between classes by which everything is interpreted. There is no overarching moral structure to creation nor a Source of truth and value which provides meaning to life or history. Where meaning exists, it is created and imposed by man himself.[9] In its assault on inequality, Marxism destroys meaning itself. Facts provide meaning and understanding, but what is a *fact* exactly? Etymologically, the word *fact* is derived from the Latin *facio*, which means to create or to design. As Rushdoony explains:

> Interpretation means the attempt to understand a given thing, something created and established; to change the world means for Marx to give a new, man-made meaning. Instead of being content with a world that is, we must remake it into the new world order made in the image of man the rebel.[10]

9. Rushdoony, *Modern Thought*, 82.

10. Ibid., 77.

Facts, meaning and knowledge are inescapably related to divine revelation, the existence and authority of which Marxism emphatically denies. There is no known fact whatsoever in the universe that is not dependent upon and mediated by either Special or General Divine Revelation. All that is true and real falls within the scope of revelation, not only on an epistemological level, but also on an ontological level, that is, reality is not only something we merely come to know and understand by revelation, but it is, for its very existence, dependent upon God as the Divine Energy or ultimate First Cause behind everything in existence. Since God is the only fully independent and self-causing Reality, all dependent realities in distinction to Him are necessarily the revelation of his thoughts and will.

At the heart of the Marxist aversion to truth and meaning is its rebellion against revelation. Deprived of all meaning, Marxism is left with a strictly materialist worldview without a moral order or absolute truth—one sanctioned by the distinctly liberal heresy of equality. For Marxists, economic inequality is directly related to the existence of private property rights and especially the fact that this property can be inherited by progeny. Socialism then proceeds to expropriate private property and other means of production, in order to collectively manage it on behalf of the people for the sake of equally redistributing the economic fruits of those means of production in an attempt to create economic equality. This is a strategy fundamentally based in the anti-Christian and anti-covenantal worldview of Marxism. The Bible, after all, teaches the principle of and right to private property in the commandments "thou shalt not steal" and "though shalt not covet thy neighbor's house." Furthermore, the Bible expressly teaches this same principle in Proverbs 13:22: "A good man leaves an inheritance to his children's children,", and in Proverbs 19:14: "Houses and riches are an inheritance from fathers." It is evident from Scripture that the inheritance of property is integral to God's covenantal blessings as a result of intergenerational faithfulness.

Marxist economics, being based in an anti-Christian worldview, is at odds with the inescapable economic laws designed by our Creator. Like Liberalism, Marxism also disregards the true nature of man as created being. Whereas the farmer or entrepreneur would walk the extra mile to save or improve his business, socialism kills initiative by reducing the entire population to the status of government wage-slaves. In such a system, all profits that would have been made are simply redistributed, and in doing so Marxism punishes diligence and hard work while rewarding laziness. In this regard Marxism does the exact opposite of what is required of government by God, namely to punish godlessness and reward obedience to God's Law (Romans 13:3-4).

While there has been a number of economic

theories proposed by Christians (e.g. Capitalism, Distributism, Physiocracy etc.), all of these have one thing in common which sharply distinguishes them from Marxism: the recognition of the right to private property and the fruits of one's own labor. The principle of private property is especially important in light of 2 Thessalonians 3:10: "If anyone will not work, neither shall he eat." This verse amplifies the Christian principle of labor as not merely an economic activity but a means of glorifying God by fulfilling the dominion mandate of Genesis 1:28. In other words, our work, whether we sweep streets or work as actuarial scientists, should in itself be done well for the purpose of serving and glorifying God.

Liberalism had achieved its great political breakthrough in 1789 in France. This initiated what many historians describe as the "long nineteenth century," which concluded with the First World War. Marxism itself achieved its greatest political breakthrough at the very end of that "long nineteenth century," with yet another anti-Christian revolution: the Bolshevik Revolution of 1917. At the start of the twentieth century there emerged a similar socio-political, philosophical and revolutionary resistance to Christianity in Russia as the one in France just over a century earlier—but this time based in Marxism itself.

The Bolshevik Revolution

Like eighteenth-century Enlightenment Liberalism culminated in the French Revolution, classical Marxism culminated in the Bolshevik Revolution of 1917. Russia was historically governed by a monarch, whom they called the "Tsar." The tsar who reigned at the start of the twentieth century, Nicholas II, the last tsar Russia would ever have, was a Christian man who holds a particularly special place in my own heart because of his support for my people during the devastating Anglo-Boer war.[11]

The reign of Tsar Nicholas II, however, was brought to an abrupt end with the Bolshevik Revolution of 1917. Like with the French Revolution, the idea of equality was once again the driving force behind this revolution, although that idea was now understood and implemented within the framework of Marxism. The catastrophic consequences of the 1917 Revolution which, believe it or not, took place in the midst of the deadly First World War, included the following:

- The Tsar and his entire family were murdered.
- According to the principles of communism, all industries and farmland were nationalized, which led to largescale poverty and even starvation.

---

11. R.W. Johnson, "Rogue's Paradise," *London Review of Books* 20(14), 1998.

- Entrepreneurs and farmers who opposed this policy of property confiscation were murdered.
- The Russian church was suppressed and the Christian religion was outlawed—state atheism replaced Russian Orthodoxy as the national religion.
- A civil war broke out even in the midst of the First World War.
- Because of starvation, persecution, and war, nearly 15 million people died during the first four years after the Bolshevik Revolution, and during the next 70 years of communism another 40 million would lose their lives due to similar reasons.[12]

It is vital to remember that all of these catastrophes were the result of apostasy from God, as the twentieth-century Russian philosopher-historian, Alexandr Solzenhitsyn explained almost 60 years after the Revolution had changed Russia permanently:

More than half a century ago, while I was still a child, I recall hearing a number of older people offer the following explanation for the great disasters that had befallen

---

12. Alexandr Solzhenitsyn, "The Templeton Address. 1983," in *In the World: Reading and Writing as a Christian*, eds. J.H, Timmerman and D.R. Hettinga (Grand Rapids, MI: Baker, 2004), 145-146.

Russia: "Men have forgotten God, and that is why all this has happened." Since then I have spent well-nigh fifty years working on the history of our Revolution; in the process I have read hundreds of books, collected hundreds of personal testimonies, and have already contributed eight volumes of my own toward the effort of clearing the rubble left by that upheaval. But if I were asked today to formulate as concisely as possible the main cause of the ruinous Revolution that swallowed up some sixty million of our people, I could not put it more accurately than to repeat: "Men have forgotten God, and that is why all this has happened.[13]

Apostasy, rebellion against God's law and design, led to this disaster. Rebellion against God is in fact at the heart of both Liberalism and Communism. Persecution of Christians as the representatives of God's kingdom was therefore also a central feature of the Soviet Communist Government. Solzhenitsyn also describes the deep regrets of Russian Christians for not having offered greater resistance as they were suffering in the forced labor camps:

How we burned in the prison camps later thinking: What would things have been

---

13. Solzhenitsyn, *Templeton*, p.145.

like if every police operative, when he went out at night to make an arrest, had been uncertain whether he would return alive? If during periods of mass arrests people had not simply sat there in their lairs, paling with terror at every bang of the downstairs door and at every step on the staircase, but had understood they had nothing to lose and had boldly set up in the downstairs hall an ambush of half a dozen people with axes, hammers, pokers, or whatever was at hand? The organs would very quickly have suffered a shortage of officers and, notwith-standing all of Stalin's thirst, the cursed machine would have ground to a halt.[14]

Thankfully communism was, from its onset, exposed to the vast majority of the people in the West as an evil and unworkable system. However, because they knew that communism would never be accepted in the Leninist-Stalinist form in the West, a group of German Marxist philosophers affiliated with Goethe University in Frankfurt in Germany, purposefully developed a new variant of Marxism in the late 1920s and early 1930s.

---

14. Alexandr Solzenhitsyn, *The Gulag Archipelago 1918–1956*, trans. T.P. Whitney (New York: Harper and Row, 2007), 13.

Cultural Marxism

The Frankfurt School, originating with a group of Marxist philosophers at the Institute for Social Research at Goethe University during the 1920s and early 1930s, desired to fundamentally reform Marxism. They proceeded to apply the Marxist emphasis on an economic class struggle to all institutions and spheres of society: marriage, the family, the church, workplace, the community, nation, and race. Here again, the Liberal principles of equality and universal brotherhood proved decisive in shaping the ideas of the Frankfurt School. The Frankfurt School variety of Marxism identified a so-called distinct aversion to otherness as historically characteristic of Western Christian Civilization. This apparent discriminating impulse, would then, according to this revised Marxist theory, serve as justification for the hatred and exclusion of those all who are different—an exclusion which then supposedly manifests itself in "racism" and "sexism"—two words coined by Frankfurt School theorists themselves during the early 1930s.[15]

At the heart of Cultural Marxism's fight against discrimination was hatred of God-given meaning and distinctions, rooted in the same egalitarianism promoted by both Liberalism and Classical Marxism. God, through His creative design, establishes meaning through differentiation. But, if all things

15. Simon Clarke, *Social Theory, Psychoanalysis and Racism* (New York: Macmillan, 2017), 79, 82.

are equal, then all things are meaningless. As Rushdoony points out: "Meaning begins with differentiation, when we say that *one* is not *fourteen*, and *nothing* is not *everything*. The equality of all things is the meaningless of all things."[16] Cultural Marxism, therefore, continues the assault upon divinely ordained realities and the divine revelation of those realities.

One of the most significant differences between the Marxist theory of the Frankfurt School and the teachings of Christianity pertains to their respective views of human relationships. Whereas Christianity views human relationships as primarily shaped by varying degrees of natural and spiritual affections and affinities (or lack thereof) (Philemon verse 17; Colossians 3:14; 2 Timothy 3:3), Marxism views all relationships as fundamentally characterized by a power struggle. The family is seen as the playing field of a power struggle between spouses and between children and parents. As two leading Frankfurt School philosophers, Theodor Adorno and Max Horkheimer described it:

> For adolescents the family no longer marks out the horizon of their lives; the autonomy of the father is vanishing and with it resistance to his authority. Earlier, the girl's servitude in the paternal home inflamed in her the passion which seemed to lead to

---

16. Rushdoony, *Modern Thought*, 59-60.

freedom but was fulfilled neither in marriage nor anywhere outside.[17]

For this perspective on the family in particular but also on human society as a whole, the Frankfurt School is of course heavily indebted to Freudian psychology.[18] In Marxism, the role of religion in society is also reduced to a means of establishing dominance in a power-relationship over the "other." In the view of the Frankfurt School, therefore, all human interaction, whether at home, at work, in social settings, or on the international stage, are fundamentally characterized by this power struggle.

Because the thinkers associated with the Frankfurt School, such as Horkheimer, Adorno, as well as Herbert Marcuse, Leo Löwenthal, and Friedrich Pollock purposefully strove to apply Marxism's original theory of a class struggle beyond the economic realm to all of society, its theory gradually became known as Cultural Marxism.[19] Its proposed solution to this struggle between different classes, genders, peoples, individuals, and races

17. Adorno & Horkheimer, *Dialectic*, 84.

18. Robert Schuett, *Political Realism, Freud and Human Nature in International Relations: The Resurrection of the Realist Man* (London: Palgrave Macmillan, 2010), 114.

19. Robert Hollinger, *Postmodernism and the Social Sciences: A Thematic Approach* (Thousand Oaks, CA: Sage, 1994), 49, 81.

lies in the dissolution of these so-called "structures of power." Cultural Marxism therefore does not take their primary aim, like classical Marxism had, at private property as such, but at the family, the church, and the nation.

Now the great irony of Cultural Marxism lies in its chosen strategy for promoting its ideology—in the name of fighting "power structures" or "institutionalized oppression," Cultural Marxists actually knowingly and deliberately infiltrated the most influential institutions of Western society, including the public schools, universities, the media, and even the churches, in order to use these structures and institutions to promote its anti-Christian ideology. Yet rather ironically this godchild of Liberalism which does not even recognize the reality of the love between a husband and wife, parents and children, or between neighbors as essential to shaping human relationships, came to use buzzwords such as "love," "tolerance," and "harmony" in its propaganda. It is the effectiveness and destructiveness of these Cultural Marxist strategies of infiltration and propaganda that are the focus of the next chapter.

CHAPTER 3

Cultural Marxism's Subversive Onslaught Against Christianity

IN THE PREVIOUS chapter, we saw how both classical Marxism and Cultural Marxism historically originated from Enlightenment Liberalism and its rebellion against divine authority. We have seen how the principal ideas which had informed the rebellion against God's created order with the rise of liberalism in the eighteenth century persisted and were re-applied through the rise of Marxism in the nineteenth century and Cultural Marxism in the twentieth century.

The scholars of the Frankfurt School, in acknowledging the failures of revolutionary Marxism in the Soviet Union, came to the realization that not only a new approach, but a fundamental change in strategy was needed. Historically, this strategic turn coincided with the Frankfurt School's re-establishment in the United States in the 1930s, after its leading figures fled Germany when the Nazis came to power.[1] Cultural Marxists then fundamentally re-evaluated their strategies of public engagement.

In Russia, the Bolsheviks violently crushed the existing socio-political order in order to build their Marxist society from the ground up on the rubble of the old Christian society. However, because this was accompanied by so much bloodshed which generated great aversion towards communism in the West, Cultural Marxists actively started to employ an alternative strategy of subversion and infiltration in an attempt to undermine Western Christian culture from within. Like a trojan horse, Cultural Marxists have spent much of the past century successfully infiltrating all of the institutions in the Western world to the point where they now, to quote the paleoconservative authors Paul Weyrich and William S. Lind, "control almost every aspect of our society: the entertainment industry (the most powerful cultural force in America), music, fine arts, the media, the universities, the public schools, even many churches."[2] I would even add that since Weyrich and Bend wrote this over a decade ago, the extent of the infiltration has increased even further, to the point where Cultural Marxists now control the overwhelming majority

---

1. Joan Braune, "Who's Afraid of the Frankfurt School? 'Cultural Marxism' as an Antisemitic Conspiracy Theory," *Journal of Social Justice* 9 (2019): 2.

2. Paul Weyrich and William Lind, *The Next Conservatism* (South Bend, IN: St. Augustine's Press, 2009), 36.

of churches and denominations not only in the United States, but across the entire Western world. It is this anti-Christian movement—which has been successfully subverting all of the West's institutions for the purpose of promoting the Cultural Marxist worldview and agenda—that has become known as the Left.

But how did this happen? How is this still happening today? In order to understand our current predicament and in order to launch an effective resistance against it, we need to trace both the historical and contemporary development of this process of infiltration and subversion.

Cultural Marxists and the Entertainment Industry

Part of the reason why Jewish people were so unpopular in Germany in the 1930s was because of their role in propagating sexual immorality among the German people during the days of the Weimar Republic (1919–1933).[3] Believe it or not, in the 1920s and early 1930s in Germany a sexual revolution occurred which was characterized by homosexual emancipation, the legalization of prostitution, a transgender movement, and the

---

3. Laurie Marhoefer, *Sex and the Weimar Republic: German Homosexual Emancipation and the Rise of the Nazis* (Toronto: University of Toronto Press, 2015), 179.

most liberal abortion law in the world at the time.[4] This movement of course only gained traction in Germany by virtue of an agressive pornographic propaganda campaign similar to the one launched prior to the French Revolution by the likes of Marquis de Sade, which was discussed earlier in this book.

These same propagandists went on the offensive when they arrived in America after fleeing Nazi Germany in the 1930s. They made it their chief goal to employ the entertainment industry to manipulate mass culture and were firmly aware of the effectiveness of art, film, and music productions for propaganda purposes in both in America and Germany.[5] In his historical work entitled *An Empire of their Own: How the Jews Invented Hollywood*, the film critic Neal Gabler notes that Hollywood was, by the late 1930s, already under the "firm hold" of Marxists.[6]

And so, by taking over the American entertainment industry, Cultural Marxists brought their sexual revolution to America. As hard as it may be to believe today, Hollywood was actually once informed by Christian principles. The Motion Pic-

4. See Marhoefer, *Sex and the Weimar Republic*.

5. Steven Ross, *Working-Class Hollywood: Silent Film and the Shaping of Class in America* (Princeton, NJ: Princeton University Press, 1998), 265.

6. Neal Gabler, *An Empire of their Own: How the Jews Invented Hollywood* (New York: Anchor Books, 1988), 330.

ture Production Code (also known as the Hays Code) which existed until the 1960s—even though it had already begun to be openly violated during the 1950s—determined, among other things, that there should be no profane references to Jesus Christ in films nor any licentious or suggestive nudity in film productions.[7] The Frankfurt School and their ideological descendants, by virtue of their creation of Jewish film production companies, played a key role in the abolishment of the Hays Code, which they framed to be an anti-Semitic regulation aimed at inhibiting Jewish film producers.[8]

So much has changed since then. You can hardly watch any production from Hollywood these days that does not contain profanities, blasphemies against our Lord Jesus Christ, and the promotion of sodomy and fornication. This propaganda machine has largely been responsible for destroying our culture. Satan knows the lure of sexual immorality to depraved human beings, and by bringing this propaganda into our very homes through television, he has done immense damage to the kingdom of Christ. That the American people would ever allow Hollywood to be infiltrated and dominated by Cultural Marxists is one of the most ludicrous disasters to strike the West during the twentieth

7. Jon Lewis, *Hollywood v. Hard Core: How the Struggle over Censorship Created the Modern Film* Industry (New York: New York University Press, 2000), 301-302.

8. Mark Wheeler, *Hollywood: Politics and Society* (London: British Film Institute, 2006), 2, 51.

century. Luke Ford, an Australian-American columnist specializing in pornography, published a book in 2004 entitled *XXX-Communicated: A Rebel without a Shul*, a memoir of his time in the industry, in which he recalls a conversation he had in 1998 with Alvin Goldstein, one of the pioneers of the hardcore pornography industry in the United States. During the interview Ford asked Goldstein why Jewish people were drastically overrepresented in the pornography industry. Goldstein answered:

> The only reason that Jews are in pornography is because we believe that Christ sucks. Catholicism sucks. We don't believe in authoritarianism. Pornography thus becomes a way of defiling Christian culture and, as it penetrates to the very heart of the American mainstream—and is no doubt consumed by those very same WASPS [White Anglo-Saxon Protestants]—its subversive character becomes more charged.[9]

Goldstein could hardly have spelled out the purposes behind the Cultural Marxist infiltration and takeover of the entertainment industry in clearer terms. This takeover of the entertainment industry in general, and the rise of the pornography industry in particular, has proven to be one of the

---

9. Luke Ford, *XXX-Communicated: A Rebel without a Shul*, (Bloomington,IN: iUniverse, 2004), 69, 160.

most effective and devastating strategies of subversion ever to be employed by the left. The Marxist strategy behind it was well-explained by the former Soviet KGB propagandist Yuri Bezmerov, who in a 1983 interview noted that the main Marxist strategy of subversion employed in the Western world has been to "corrupt the young, get them interested in sex, take them away from religion... [to] cause breakdown of the old moral virtues: honesty, sobriety, self-restraint, faith in the pledged word."[10]

Think about this: even if you are married, you would never think about having sex in front of children. The thought would never cross any decent person's mind. You would never swear at God in front of children. Yet by virtue of the entertainment industry, our children are constantly exposed to nudity, sex scenes, sexually suggestive language, and profanities like "Jesus f@&%ing Christ" even in non-X-rated films. This dynamic is quite disturbing—it brings an awkwardness and tension into an otherwise safe and relaxing family environment, promotes a competing value system, and desensitizes all of us to the sexual licentiousness and anti-Christ ideology promoted by the Left. This should, if anything, stir us up with a righteous anger to the point of vehemently

---

10. Yuri Bezmerov, *Yuri Bezmenov Full Interview & Lecture – HQ* (1983), https://www.youtube.com/watch?v=pzeHpf3OYQY.

desiring and actively praying for Hollywood's complete destruction.

Totalitarianism is always preceded by moral anarchy. Therefore, promoting sexual licentiousness serves a very distinct Marxist purpose. Forsaking the supremacy of the divine, transcendent moral order as authoritative standard in favor of moral self-determination, inevitably leads to a kind of social anarchy from which government tyranny alone can offer liberation.

Another way in which the entertainment industry subverts and undermines Christian morality, is through the deliberate and constant blurring of the distinction between good and evil itself. Either consciously or subconsciously, the enemies of God know that morality can only be derived from a divine Lawgiver. Even the most ardent atheist scholars now admit that morality itself, both for the individual and as a framework for public life, requires an authoritative Lawgiver.[11] In their implicit denial or hatred of God's authority and existence, the plots of many modern films and series are therefore distinctly aimed at not only subverting Christian morality, but doing away with the very distinction between good and evil itself. This

11. Jürgen Habermas, "Constitutional Democracy: A Paradoxical Union of Contradictory Principles?" *Theoretical and Empirical Studies of Rights* (Edited by L.B. Nielson. London: Routledge, 2017), 25; Walter Sinnot-Armstrong, *Morality without God?* (Oxford: Oxford University Press, 2009), 100.

is why so many popular modern productions have such thoroughly disappointing conclusions (think of series such as *Game of Thrones* or *House of Cards*, for example). They might still have somewhat creative plots, but they are largely devoid of any meaning or purpose.

Cultural Marxists and the Media

Every once in a while, I suffer through the unfortunate experience of having to watch a mainstream news broadcast. It is rather astonishing how they manipulate the public narrative in every possible way so as to indoctrinate the masses with their anti-Christian message. To the mainstream media, white men are the perpetual antagonists—evil oppressors from which women and other races need continual liberation. Yet at the same time, the liberal Western governments in Europe and North America who slavishly follow the establishment's agenda are upheld as the standard for the world. Those who oppose the agenda of Cultural Marxism, even if it means supporting a half-liberal like Donald Trump, are mocked, ridiculed, and humiliated. The examples of media inconsistencies and blatant anti-white and anti-Christian propaganda are legion and should be evident to anyone with eyes to see (which, lamentably, it apparently is not). But for the sake of the argument, let's consider two well-known case studies:

1. The media coverage of Nick Sandmann's actions during the 2019 March for Life.
2. The arrest and death of George Floyd in May 2020.

In January 2019, the annual March for Life took place in opposition to the United States' genocidal abortion laws that have led to the murder of over 60 million babies. Among the participants were a group of students from Covington Catholic High School in Park Hills, Kentucky. After the march, while waiting for their bus, the students were intimidated by a liberal, pro-abortion Native American activist named Nathan Phillips. One of the students, Nicholas Sandmann stood his ground in the midst of the attempted intimidation from Phillips, but the media spectacularly portrayed Sandmann, a white Catholic boy of 17, as the perpetrator of a hate crime simply for refusing to back down. As a result, Sandmann settled lawsuits worth hundreds of millions with the Washington Post and CNN.[12]

There was no such justice for Derek Chauvin, the police officer who was unjustly convicted of murdering George Floyd. The jury's decision was certainly influenced by the media's narrative that was based on lies, deception, and suppression of evidence. Floyd, a violent criminal who once phys-

12. Alex Marlow, *Breaking the News: Exposing the Establishment Media's Hidden Deals and Secret Corruption* (New York: Simon & Schuster, 2021), 263.

ically threatened to kill a pregnant woman and her baby while robbing their home, died in May 2020 during arrest after using a counterfeit $20 bill at a store in Minnesota. Chauvin was convicted of murder, but as social commentator Ann Coulter points out:

> the hostile crowd itself prevented the officers from attempting to perform CPR in the last minutes of Floyd's life... Even the prosecution's "use of force" experts admitted repeatedly on cross-examination that a hostile crowd would justify Chauvin keeping Floyd restrained until an ambulance arrived. An officer's duty to provide care is overridden by his duty to keep himself, the suspect and the bystanders safe. As was evident from the videos (and admitted to by the bystander witnesses), they were shouting obscenities at the police, threatening them with bodily harm and, in a few instances, had to be held back from rushing the officers. And of course, because of the presence of the angry crowd, the EMTs themselves did not stick around to provide care, but did a "load and scoot," heaving Floyd into the back of the ambulance and driving three blocks to get away from the mob on the street. They didn't even want to work inside an ambulance near this feisty group. [I]t becomes increasingly obvious that the

belligerent onlookers themselves may have gotten George Floyd killed by creating a dangerous situation for the officers.[13]

Furthermore, the jury, under the spell of a false media narrative, simply completely ignored the testimony of the former chief medical examiner of Maryland, Dr. David Fowler, who testified that Floyd died because of heart failure rather than police restraint.[14]

The same lying and deceptive tactics were evident throughout the mainstream media's justification of the tyrannical measures and mandates imposed during the Covid-19 pandemic. Despite the fact that peer-reviewed studies by researchers from premier research universities found that ivermectin and hydroxychloroquine are both safe and effective treatments for Covid-19 and that even mild cases of Covid-19 can lead to lifelong immunity,[15] these findings were completely ignored by the

13. Ann Coulter, "Derek Chauvin, George Floyd, and the Case against Mob justice," *Breitbart* (April 14, 2021), https://www.breitbart.com/politics/2021/04/14/ann-coulter-derek-chauvin-george-floyd-and-the-case-against-mob-justice/.

14. Rachael Alexander, "Chauvin defence witness testifies George Floyd died due to heart issues," *The Independent* (April 15, 2021), https://www.independent.ie/world-news/north-america/chauvin-defence-witness-testifies-george-floyddied-due-to-heart-issues-40314599.html.

15. Chadwick Podromos and Tobias Rumschlag, "Hydroxychloroquine is effective, and consistently so

mainstream media, as well as the scientific estab-lishment. Ironically, the media was adamant that the widespread Black Lives Matter protests fol-lowing the death of George Floyd—which openly violated the very lockdown measures they so vehe-mently promoted at the time—did not contribute to the spread of Covid-19 infections.[16]

The media's absolute and shameless hatred of traditional Christian civilization, as embodied by the European peoples in Europe, North America, Aus-tralasia, and Southern Africa, now features in almost every report and program that the establishment media produces. Why? Because Cultural Marxists dominate the media industry and have successfully taken over almost all of the big media corporations and actively employ these for their ends.

---

when provided early, for COVID-19: a systematic review," *New Microbes New Infections* 38:100776 (November 2021): doi: 10.1016/j.nmni.2020.100776; Jackson Turner, Wooseob Kim, Elizaveta Kalaidina, Charles Gloss, Adri-ana Rauseo, Aaron Schmitz, Lena Hansen, Alem Haile, Michael Klebert, Iskra Pusic, Jane O'Halloran, Rachel Presti, Ali Ellebedy, "SARS-CoV-2 infection induces long-lived bone marrow plasma cells in humans," *Nature* (2021), https://doi.org/10.1038/s41586-021-03647-4. As of December 2021, Ivermectin has been proven to be effective against Covid-19 by more than 60 peer-reviewed studies, which can all be accessed at https://ivmmeta.com/.

16. Ken Coleman, "Report: BLM Protests Have Not Contributed to Covid-19 Spread," *MSN* (September 7, 2020), https://www.msn.com/en-us/news/us/report-blm-protests-have-not-contributed-to-covid-19-spread/ar-BB16wNM9.

Cultural Marxists, the Public
Schools, and the Universities

Imagine believing that you are being a responsible Christian parent fulfilling your covenantal duties by sending your child to be trained up in a Humanist and Cultural Marxist worldview in public school for 30 hours per week and thinking that 45 minutes of weekly Sunday school classes will be sufficient to endow your child with a Christian worldview. Such a strategy is evidently doomed because the public school system in most Western countries is completely and utterly godless—a natural reflection of the governments to which these school systems are responsible. Yet sadly, many Christian parents still attempt it nonetheless.

Public Schools are also inefficient when it comes to the purpose of their design (to provide children with an education), as they often simply lower their standards in the name of equality, which has become the central religious principle that informs their educational philosophy.[17] Furthermore, no matter how dedicated the teachers are, it is impossible to provide children with a quality education as long as the educational philosophy underlying the curriculum is completely flawed. While the old Enlightenment ideal of "objectivity" in science, research, and education has now been widely dis-

17. Christopher Klicka, *Home Schooling: The Right Choice: An Academic, Historical, Practical and Legal Perspective* (Bend, OR: Loyal Publishing, 2000), 34.

carded in academia,[18] public education still seems to be caught up in nineteenth-century humanism. One of the Enlightenment ideas central to the philosophical behaviorism underlying modern public education is the outdated concept of the mind as a "clean slate."[19] This is based largely on the Enlightenment ideal of liberation from God and from history, by which the mind is conceived of as an empty container or a blank paper to be filled with ideas through education. But because this ideal is so radically at odds with reality—after all, all of us are born with distinct talents and dispositions—the duty of the teacher essentially becomes to attempt to usurp the role of God and remake the student into the humanist image. As Rushdoony explains:

> The concept of the mind as a clean tablet was very quickly exploded as a psychological reality but it remained as an ideal... This concept dominated all thinking in the French Revolution and extended itself to the point of beginning again in the reckoning of time. It was basic to the thinking of all the anarchists, Marxists such as Lenin and others... [I]t has provided the ideal for scientific thinking. The true scientist

18. David Carr, *Historical Experience: Essays on the Phenomenology of History* (Routledge: New York, 2021), 7.

19. Rushdoony, *Intellectual Schizophrenia*, 2.

ostensibly wipes his mind free of all precon-
ceptions and approaches his subject with a
clean-tablet mind... This scientific attitude
is one of the great myths of modern times.[20]

Indeed, the ideal of the Marxist system of
education currently prevalent in public schools
throughout the Western world is not only unprac-
tical but fundamentally destructive. As the Dutch
Reformed philosopher Herman Dooyeweerd
(1894—1977) has righty pointed out, the reality
of theoretical thought is such that presuppositions
or pre-theoretical axioms necessarily underpin all
human thought and that these presuppositions, by
virtue of their epistemological nature and as spiritual driving forces impelling any thinker to interpret
reality through its lenses, always and inescapably
have a distinctly religious significance.[21] This is
because the axiomatic nature of human thought
pertains to the innate human impulse to direct itself
towards the absolute origin, source, and cause of all
meaning, and as such these inescapable presuppositions are non-demonstrable commitments taken
on faith.[22] It is precisely because of its failure to
understand the very nature of human thought, that

---

20. Ibid., 3.

21. Herman Dooyeweerd, *De wijsbegeerte der
wetsidee. Boek I: De wetsidee als grondlegging der wijsbegeerte* (Amsterdam: H.J. Paris, 1935), vi-vii.

22. Ibid., 21, 24.

Rushdoony notes that the behaviorist educational philosophy underlying the liberal public education system is rooted in the idea of "the deliverance from meaning to method," that is, liberal education aims at creating its own meaning through method.[23] And that man-made meaning, apart from being a distortion of the truth as revealed by God, also serves to enslave us and our children to the god-state.

Additionally, by sending children to spend more social and educational time with their secular peers and teachers in a public school than they do at home, we are grooming them for the world, slavery to sin, and the punishment of death that accompanies being attached to a godless world. If there was ever a perfect strategy invented for ensuring the apostasy of our children, this would be it. When the entire philosophy of education which shapes the curricula of public schools is based in Cultural Marxism, as is the case today, there can simply be no legitimate argument for sending Christian children to anti-Christian public schools. Parents have a covenantal obligation to ensure that their children are educated in the ways of the Lord (Deuteronomy 6:7). This covenantal obligation is also accompanied by a divine promise. In Proverbs 22:6 we read: "Train up a child in the way he should go, and when he is old he will not depart from it." Apostasy is

---

23. Rousas John Rushdoony, *The Messianic Character of American Education: Studies in the History of the Philosophy of Education* (Vallecito, CA: Ross House, 1995), 311.

never the result of God's failure to deliver on his promises. Apostasy is always the result of man's failure to fulfill his covenantal obligations.

The general population's reaction to the Covid-19 lockdowns is a fine example of how public education has killed people's ability to think critically and turned them into slaves. As mentioned earlier, scientific studies have shown that the lockdowns and masks do not work.[24] And while more than a few may know this to be true (after all, how many people do you actually know who had not violated a number of lockdown measures?), only a very small part of the general population refuses to suppress that knowledge. For the sake of being socially accepted, for the sake of not being ridiculed as a conspiracy theorist, or for whatever other reason, the vast majority of people—including the scientific establishment—simply refuse to believe the scientific evidence and prefer to follow the mainstream media and government narrative. Why is this? Because they have been schooled in the government religion and have come to accept it wholesale. The same way we as Christians believe in the infallibility of the Bible as Word of God, government school educated people believe in the infallibility of the mainstream media as the infallible word of the god-state.

An American friend once suggested to me per-

---

24. Klompas et. al., *Universal Masking*: 1-3; Brendavit et al., *Mandatory Stay-at-Home and Business Closure Effects*: 1-9.

haps one of the most important reasons why the Right is losing the culture war: despite the fact that the conservative half of America is having lots of kids and the liberals are having almost none, the problem is that the conservatives are sending their kids to be educated by the liberals and thereby the liberals are winning through converting all the conservatives' children to their cause.[25] The same thing can sadly also happen even when children are homeschooled or sent to private Christian schools but are not thoroughly equipped with a comprehensive Christian worldview able to resist mainstream propaganda.

This is true throughout the West. When I had lived in the Netherlands while working on my PhD, I used to closely follow the annual reports of the membership figures of the various Dutch Reformed churches in the country. The mainline denominations showed a consistently increasing decline every year for obvious reasons. I mean, why would anyone get out of bed on a Sunday morning and go through the effort of going to church if you can get the same message by simply switching on your television? The conservative denominations,

---

25. This is of course not the main reason why the Right is losing the culture war, but it might be second only to the government policy of allowing mass immigration from the third-world. Through this policy the Left not only demographically replaces the white populations of Western nations in order to undermine their social cohesion and Christian cultures, but also literally imports their own voters.

on the other hand, have tended to grow marginally every year over the past couple of decades. But do not be fooled that this is a good sign. It is not. It is commonplace for conservative Reformed families in the Netherlands to have, on average, 4 to 6 children. This means that even if the churches never reached a single secular individual by virtue of their missionary efforts, their numbers would double with every generation simply by virtue of a natural, covenantal increase. But their real increase does not even come close to a fraction of that. And the reason is because the secular world swallows up nearly half the Christian children in the Netherlands. The idea that you can live in a society where the covenantal apostasy rate is around 50% and think that you are doing an okay job is absolutely senile. It shows to what extent we have forsaken our covenantal obligations, because God surely has not forsaken his covenantal promises (see Proverbs 22:6 and Isaiah 49:25). What makes this reality even worse is the fact that the majority of children born into conservative Reformed households in the Netherlands also attend Christian (often Reformed) schools. This just goes to show how even private Christian schools often lack a rigorous and consistent Christian curriculum with a comprehensive worldview education and remain vulnerable to the interventionist state's secular agenda.

The Left's infiltration of our education system has been so thorough, that they nowadays have all their bases covered. After all, if the school system will not indoctrinate children sufficiently, the university is sure to get them as young adults. I attended a private Calvinist Christian school as a boy. After graduating high school, many of my peers and I took the next logical step to go enroll for studies at the local university. What astonished me is that after a year or so, most of my peers who had been educated through our school's Christian curriculum had, to a large degree, actually embraced the secular worldview of their professors and fellow-students. The pressure seemed to get to them. Young Christian men and women face intense social pressure in college. The freedom and atomization cultivated by campus culture amounts to a licentiousness that has no correlation to true liberty in Christ. The drunken parties and sexual immorality promoted by this culture enslaves one to the most primitive and depraved urges, and it is in fact quite contrary to fostering a culture of innovation and disciplined free-thought that is supposed to characterize the university setting. Peer-pressure plays an immense role in the satanic plan to corrupt the souls of the youth by means of integrating them in this depraved culture. But the satanic Leftist plan aimed at the corruption of the youth extends even to the classroom itself.

Back in 2008, I was a freshman in college taking a course in Old Testament theology. During class, our professor claimed that none of the Old Testament texts that prophesy of the coming of Christ in the flesh was actually about Christ. Rather, they were about some other figure who lived in the historical context when the prophets were writing. Yes, imagine that—Isaiah was referring not to Christ, but to some unknown and relatively random and obscure figure in the ancient Near East in the eighth century BC when he spoke about the Child being born and called "Wonderful, Counselor, Mighty God, Everlasting Father, Prince of Peace" (Isaiah 9:6)! This is, of course, beyond absurd. But this interpretation now passes as mainstream scholarship and the professor was able to convince more than 90% of our class of its orthodoxy. The history of the past few decades testifies to the immense successes achieved by the Cultural Marxists by means of their slow march through the educational institutions. Back in the late 1950s, when the former president of Yale University, professor Whitney Griswold, defended a liberal philosophy of education by claiming that "the voice of the people is the voice of God,"[26] South African Calvinist intellectuals shuddered at the fact that a formerly Reformed Christian institution such as Yale had turned humanistic. Yet by 2015 the rector of my own *alma mater*, the University of the Free State in South Africa, openly referred to the "Calvinist god" as a "violent, sectarian god… a racist construction of the divine." [27]

---

26. A Whitney Griswold, *Liberal Education and the Democratic Ideal and other Essays* (New Haven, CT: Yale University Press, 1959), 99.

27. Jonathan Jansen, *Leading for Change: Race, Inti-*

Given these realities that characterize the modern university and the Cultural Marxist worldview that informs its curricula, is it any wonder then that even most medical professionals today are unable to distinguish true science from false government narratives? Is it any wonder that most clergy are ill-equipped to address the major threats to the Christian church and Christian orthodoxy in our day? Is it any wonder that even legal professionals have been unable and unwilling to uphold our historical, constitutional, and biblical rights against the Left's agenda of reinventing the entire Western legal system in accordance with their diabolical designs? Is it any wonder that economists remain silent and simply do not seem to care when the national debt skyrockets and the dept-to-GDP ratio becomes unsustainable or when reserve banks devaluate all of our money through Quantitative easing? However, if the Left does not win you over at school or at university and even if you shelter yourself and your children from Hollywood movies, the secular media and public schools, they will make sure to get you at church.

Cultural Marxists and the Churches

Of all the institutions that the Cultural Marxists have successfully infiltrated, perhaps none has

---

macy and Leadership on divided University Campuses (London: Routledge, 2015), 101.

served their aim of subverting Christianity as much as the institutional church itself. Cultural Marxists weren't the first Marxists to try infiltrate the church to promote their devilish agenda. This had already been attempted in nineteenth-century France by the likes of Socialists such as Phillippe Buchez and Etienne Cabet, although without notable success.[28] Historically, the Cultural Marxist infiltration of the churches proceeded by means of the theological seminaries—a strategy deliberately employed by the left throughout both the twentieth and twenty-first centuries.

At the dawn of the twentieth century, there was a battle for the heart of Christianity brewing in American Presbyterianism. In what would become known as the Fundamentalist-Modernist controversy, conservative Presbyterians fought vehemently against the false doctrines denying the authority of Scripture, the unity of the Old and New Testaments, and the resurrection of Jesus Christ. This source of this controversy was the spread of Higher Criticism from Germany to the United States during the nineteenth century. Higher Criticism, based upon the liberal presupposition that the authority of human reason trumps that of divine revelation, was promoted in the United States by the likes of the Hebrew scholar Charles Briggs (1841–1913), who had studied in Germany. According to Briggs, the text of the Old Testament

---

28. Webster, *World Revolution*, 109-111, 115.

in particular reflected a lower view of morality than that which Enlightened man had acquired by the nineteenth century.[29] This attack on the authority of Scripture was rooted in the liberal hermeneutics of German rationalists such as Friedrich Schleiermacher (1768–1834). Schleiermacher built upon the rationalist re-definition of the idea of *Divine Accommodation* proposed by the seventeenth-century Dutch Cartesian theologian, Christoph Wittich. Divine Accommodation, properly understood, is an orthodox doctrine that has been held by theologians since the early church. St. Augustine, for example, understood Divine Accommodation as the Holy Spirit's use of anthropomorphic expressions[30] for the purpose of revealing God's character and will in an understandable way to fallible and limited human beings. In other words, within the Augustinian theological tradition, Divine Accommodation is understood as a concession made by God Himself to the limited understanding capabilities of human beings.[31] In Genesis 22:12, for example, the Lord, after first commanding Abra-

---

29. Gary Dorrien, *The Making of American Liberal Theology: Imagining Progressive Religion 1805–1900* (Louisville: Westminster/John Knox, 2001), 358-359.

30. An anthropomorphism is defined as the attribution of human traits and emotions to non-human entities, in this particular case God.

31. Arnold Huijgen, *Divine accommodation in John Calvin's theology: Analysis and assessment* (Göttingen: Vandenhoek & Ruprecht, 2011), 86.

ham to offer his son, only to stop him from actually
committing the act, proceeds to tell Abraham that
"now I know that you fear God, since you have
not withheld your son, your only son, from Me."
In his commentary on this verse John Calvin writes
the following:

> How can anything become known to God
> in time, since the knowledge of all things
> is always present with Him? Truly, it is
> because God here accommodates Himself
> to the level of mere mortals, that He here
> says that that which has now been revealed
> by experience, has become known to Him.
> And God often speaks to us not in accor-
> dance with his endless wisdom, but in
> accordance with our weaknesses.[32]

Calvin's understanding of Divine Accommodation, as is evident from this text, therefore confirms
the church historian Jon Balserak's claim that the
reformer "rarely, if ever, suggests a conception of
the Bible which understands its truth as being his-

---

32. John Calvin, *In primum Mosis librum, qui genesis
vulgo dicitur commentarius* (Robert Stephanus: Geneva,
1554), 162. This is my own translation from the original
Latin, which reads: "quomodo aliquid Deo innotescit, cui
semper omnia fuerut praesentia? Nepe hominu moribus
se conformas, quod experimento probavit, sibi nunc dicit
esse cognitu. Neque enim pro immesa sua sapientia, sed
pro nostra infirmitate nobiscu loquitur".

torically-relative, as seems to have been the case with later proponents of accommodation."[33]

What most church historians, including even the world-renowned specialist in Protestant thought after the Reformation, Richard A. Muller, have missed, however, is the true impact of the seventeenth-century semantic change which occurred with regard to the concept of Divine Accommodation under the influence of Enlightenment rationalism.[34] As a liberal Dutch rationalist theologian, Christoph Wittich (1625–1687) re-applied the notion in an unprecedented way: for Wittich the biblical text itself reflected the so-called misconceptions and prejudices of both its human author and first audience—misconceptions that could be overcome by the right use of human reason. Biblical texts were, to Wittich, always subject to epistemic suspicion and remain dubious until and only if they are ratified by human reason.[35] Wittich's rational-

33. Jon Balserak, *Divinity Compromised: A Study of Divine Accommodation in the Thought of John Calvin* (Dordtrecht: Springer, 2006), 8-9.

34. Muller wrongly attributes the rise of the modernist understanding of Divine Accommodation as "a use of time-bound and even erroneous statements as a medium for revelation" to the eighteenth-century German rationalist Lutheran, Johann Semmler. See Richard Muller, *Dictionary of Latin and Greek Theological Terms: Drawn Principally from Protestant Scholastic Theology* (Grand Rapids, MI: Baker, 2006), 19.

35. Christoph Wittich, *Consensus veritatis in scriptura divina et infallibili revelatae cum veritate philosophica a*

ist philosophy, firmly rooted in Enlightenment liberalism, thereby laid the foundations for the Theological Liberalism and especially the higher criticism of the nineteenth century as it was embodied by the likes of Reverend Briggs, who ultimately argued for the authority of man over that of God and His revelation. It also helped shape the social gospel promoted early in the twentieth century by denominations such as the Methodist Episcopal Church in the United States,[36] which itself was an inversion of Christian morality, and while borrowing biblical concepts, emptied them of their meaning so as to promote a materialist, egalitarian, and socialist worldview among believers.

This strategy was central to the Theological Liberalism that the so-called "fundamentalist" Presbyterian school rightly opposed. One of the leading representatives of this school, John Gresham Machen (1881–1937), a professor of New Testament at Princeton Theological Seminary, noted at the time that "the chief modern rival of Christianity is Liberalism. An examination of the teachings of Liberalism in comparison with those of Christian-

---

Renato DesCartes detecta (Boutensteyn & Lever: Leiden, 1682), 297.

36. Christopher Evans, *The Social Gospel in American Religion: A History* (New York University Press: New York), 90.

ity will show that at every point the two movements are in direct opposition."[37]

Machen thus rightly understood that these two religions are fundamentally at odds with each other. After all, the Liberals who had infiltrated the seminaries and churches in Machen's time denied all the core doctrines of Christianity: the authority of Scripture, the virgin birth and historical-bodily resurrection of Jesus Christ, as well as God's Lordship as Ruler and Lawgiver over all creation. And behind the promotion of this so-called "Liberal Christianity" in Machen's time there was already the hidden hand of Cultural Marxism.

In 1996 the Christian Reconstructionist author Gary North published one of his most important and valuable books, entitled *Crossed Fingers: How the Liberals Captured the Presbyterian Church*. While focusing on the history of a particular denomination, the Presbyterian Church (USA), it essentially addresses the same issue as this book: North himself notes that his book is very much "about a conflict between two mighty religions, Christianity and humanism."[38] The work is undoubtedly valuable. It is worth reading. However, it is quite astonishing that in a 1,100 page monograph on the conflict between Christianity

37. John G. Machen, *Christianity and Liberalism* (MacMillan: New York, 1923), 53.

38. Gary North, *Crossed Fingers: How the Liberals captured the Presbyterian Church* (Tyler, TX: Institute for Christian Economics, 1996), xviii.

and a false religion rooted in the Enlightenment idea of human sovereignty, North actually manages to mention Marxism only thrice: twice he wrongly lists it alongside nationalism as one the fruits of rationalism,[39] making the only sensible reference to Marxism in the entire book a brief comment about how it shares with Liberalism an aversion to agrarianism.[40] For whatever reason, North's work is clearly lacking in one vital aspect: it fails to address what has for nearly a century been the central driving force behind not only the destruction of the Presbyterian Church (USA) but Western Christendom as a whole. For example, in Machen's own day the Cultural Marxist John D. Rockefeller (1839–1937), a wealthy American businessman, founded and heavily financed a whole army of liberal theological movements and institutions that played a central role in the promotion of "Liberal

---

39. Ibid., 154, 761. Ironically, the very term "nationalism" was originally coined by the Counter-Enlightenment philosopher-historian Johann Gottfried Herder (1744–1803), who conceived of it as merely a continuation of the traditional Christian social ontology in which the nation is ultimately an extended family. He therefore argues that the borders of states should correspond with the living spaces of the respective ethnicities as opposed to the liberal ideal in which the state can be imperially expanded based on the Enlightenment fantasy of a social contract. See my article entitled "The Role of Familialism in Counter-Enlightenment Social Ontology" published in the *Journal for Christian Scholarship* 57(3-4) (2021), 135-147.

40. Ibid., 573.

Christianity," such as the University of Chicago, the Interchurch World Movement, the Institute of Social and Religious Research, and various liberal professors at Union Theological Seminary.[41]

All of Rockefeller's activities were in line with the Cultural Marxist strategy, aimed at the subversion and destruction of true Christianity. While most Cultural Marxists do not care for doctrinal disputes within Christianity, they have no problem promoting Liberalism for the purpose of subverting and ultimately destroying what they have rightly identified to be its greatest enemy, Christ's Church Militant.

They have not forsaken this strategy by any means since the time of Machen. In fact, they have gradually grown in confidence and audacity. By 1953, the anti-communist counterintelligence agent, Herbert Philbrick, wrote an article for the *Christian Herald* in which he revealed that he knows that

the Reds have planted secret Communists in pulpits, how they have infiltrated the seminaries, how they 'use' good and unsus-

---

41. Robert M. Miller, "John D. Rockefeller Jr.: An Exchange," *New York Review* (15 July 2004), https://www.nybooks.com/articles/2004/07/15/john-d-rockefeller-jr-an-exchange/. For an explanation of the Rockefeller family's affinity for the Cultural Marxism of the Frankfurt School, see Austin Rose, *Fake Science: Exposing the Left's skewed statistics, fuzzy facts, and dodgy data* (Regnery: Washington, DC, 2017), 89.

pecting Protestants, Catholics... you will realize that subversion in the sanctuary is the most deadly and insidious menace facing America today, so that you will not only be aware of the danger but be prepared to counteract it.[42]

Philbrick identifies one of their core strategies as being the infiltration of the seminaries, thereby "prostituting the Christian ministry to the evil ends of atheism."[43] He proceeds to explain, by means of an example, how the subversion worked in practice at the time:

"Mass meetings" are always important to Communist Party agitators, and the use of religious leaders here is very helpful to the Reds. A Sunday, January 16, 1953, meeting held in New York City is typical of hundreds of similar ones conducted every month across the country. A group calling itself the "National Committee to Defend Negro Leadership" presented citations to "Negro

---

42. Herbert Philbrick, "The Communists are After Your Church: A Reprint on Mr. Philbrick's Article for the Christian Herald," *Communist Methods of Infiltration: Hearings before the Committee of Un-American Activities in the House of Representatives, eighty-third Congress, First Session* (Washington, DC: United States Government Printing Office, 1953), 2019.

43. Ibid., 2021.

men and women who have fought for democracy and peace"—noble objectives in anybody's book... A minister delivered the invocation and was chairman of the citation committee. All this, however, was only "cover" for the principle objective of the meeting: to build and promote the prestige and standing of top Communist Party bosses. The chief address was delivered by an editor of the official Communist Party publication, *Masses and Mainstream*.[44]

Cultural Marxists gradually shifted their strategy from promoting Liberal "Christianity" to promoting downright Cultural Marxism within even the traditionally conservative denominations. Take the conservative Presbyterian Church in America (PCA), for example. This denomination was started by conservative Southern Presbyterians who became fed-up with the Liberalism of the of the Presbyterian Church in the United States, from which it separated in 1973. In fact, one of the founding members of the PCA, John Edward Richards, wrote in his work concerning the reasons for the separation that the growing influence of Marxism in the Presbyterian Church in the United States was one of the most important and decisive reasons for the split. Richards identifies non-Christian ideologies of "oneness" prevalent within the Presbyterian

44. Ibid., 2023-2024.

Church in the United States, including that of the "Socialist, who declares all men are equal. Therefore, there must be a great leveling of humanity and a oneness of privilege and possession," as well as that of the "Communist, who would have one mass of humanity coerced into oneness by a totalitarian state and guided exclusively by Marxist philosophy."[45] Yet somehow, within merely four decades of the split, the most influential figure in the PCA would be a Cultural Marxist himself. In his well-known book, *The Reason for God*, Tim Keller, former pastor at Redeemer Presbyterian Church and faculty member at Westminster Theological Seminary in Philadelphia, readily admits that his theology and ethics has been greatly shaped by the Cultural Marxism of the Frankfurt School, more so than by the theological sources he had studied at seminary. Keller writes that as a student in the late 1960s, he found the "social activism [of the neo-Marxist Frankfurt School] particularly attractive and the critique of American bourgeoisie society compelling" even if the school's "philosophical underpinnings were confusing" to him at the time. Yet, for him it was the Cultural Marxists of the 1960s, not the Christians, who were "most passionate about social justice."[46] The impact of

---

45. John E. Richards, *The Historical Birth of the Presbyterian Church in America* (Liberty Hill, SC: The Liberty Press, 1987), 57.

46. Timothy J. Keller, *The Reason for God* (London: Hodder & Stoughton, 2009), xi-xii.

Cultural Marxism in shaping Keller's theological framework is evidenced in a December 2021 tweet, where Keller stated that "[t]he heart of the gospel is the cross, and the cross is all about giving up power."[47] Of course after being rightly criticized he tried to explain away the heresy in follow-up tweets by pointing out how Jesus refrained from using his power on the cross, but it is obvious that surrendering power and refraining from using it are two entirely different things. The fact of the matter is that Keller, like the Marxists, interprets all reality within the framework of a power struggle—even to the point of blasphemously redefining Christ's work of redemption within this Marxist framework.

The contemporary African-American Reformed theologian Voddie Baucham therefore rightly identifies Keller, along with other prominent American clergy such as Thabiti Anyabwile, Russell Moore, and organizations such as The Gospel Coalition and Together for the Gospel (T4G), as subverters of the gospel dedicated to the promotion of the Frankfurt School's Cultural Marxism within the American institutional church.[48]

I would actually go further than Baucham, how-

---

47. Timothy Keller, Twitter, December 19, 2021, 7:30 pm, https://twitter.com/timkellernyc/status/1472620245491896324.

48. Voddie T. Baucham, *Fault Lines: The Social Justice Movement and Evangelicalism's Looming Catastrophe* (Washington, DC: Salem Books, 2021), 2, 208.

ever, in that I think the corruption of the clergy's theology via the influence of Cultural Marxism—albeit often unknowingly and unintentionally—is even more prevalent than he realizes. It is not just those who rage about the mythical threat of "white supremacy" or promote Critical Race Theory who are openly subverting the church, but all advocates of the heresy of egalitarianism who have, unfortunately, fallen victim to the propaganda of Cultural Marxist sympathizers such as Tim Keller through the seminaries and the churches. The Cultural Marxist social justice promoted by these clergy is a radical subversion of the biblical concept of justice rooted in God's nature and revelation of his will. Whereas egalitarian social justice always favors the poor over the rich, the weak over the strong, the lazy over the industrious, and the oppressed (real or imagined) over the privileged (real or imagined), biblical justice aims to regulate relationships in a way that is fair to both parties, without showing favoritism based on talents, socio-economic status, race, or sex (Leviticus 19:34; Matthew 25:29; Acts 10:34). Even more significantly, as we noted in chapter 2, egalitarianism entails a complete loss of meaning, which can only be truly provided by the creative and redemptive work of Christ. As Bavinck points out, the work of Christ redeems nature and God-given realities, without levelling, destroying or absorbing them.[49]

---

49. Bavinck, *Handleiding*, 116.

But this of course begs the inevitable question of how this came to be. How did it happen that the Left has managed to, within a couple of decades following World War II, almost completely subvert all of our institutions, including even the conservative ecclesiastical institutions? How did the church not realize, react and stop this in time? How have our enemies managed to completely subvert and destroy nearly all that our ancestors worked so hard to build up? Where exactly did we slip up? Answering these questions will be the focus of our next chapter.

CHAPTER 4

How the Current Crisis Came to Be

IN THE WESTERN world, there is simply no denying the reality that, as things stand today the Left
has largely succeeded in achieving the core aims of
their strategies of subversion aimed at Christianity. The fruits of their successes are evident in the
wholesale acceptance of Egalitarianism by the vast
majority of professing Christians. Yet Egalitarianism, the central doctrine of Liberalism, is based on
Marxism's foundational hatred of Christ. The ideas
and theories of Marxism are being promoted—
consciously and unconsciously—from pulpits all
across the globe, but in the West in particular.
Given Christ's promise that the Gates of Hell will
never prevail against the true church (Matthew
16:18), however, it follows that this could only
have happened because the church has forsaken the
truth and strength of the gospel. It could only have
happened if the vigor of the Church Militant has
been ripped away from us by false doctrines and

practices. The ways in which the church has failed, the manner in which she has been neutered, and the heresies in our own midst that have enabled all of this destruction, are the focus of this chapter. First, we will take a look at the impact of the heresies relating to the Neo-Gnosticism prevalent in the modern church. Then we will focus on the false doctrine of Radical Two Kingdom Theology (also known as "Reformed two kingdoms").

Neo-Gnosticism

In order to understand the roots of Neo-Gnosticism, as well as its impact on weakening and neutering the church, we need to take a brief look at the old Gnosticism which plagued the ancient church during the first few centuries after Christ. Two of the central tenets of Gnosticism are the denial of the authority of divine revelation and an aversion towards reality as creation of God.[1] The term itself is derived from the Greek γνωστικός, *(gnostikos)* meaning "to have knowledge." This refers to Gnosticism's fundamental epistemic doctrine that true knowledge comes from the inner enlightenment of the human mind itself, to the exclusion of the external illumination of the Holy Spirit. Its similarities with the rationalism of the Enlightenment are striking, as is its historical use of

---

1. Rousas J. Rushdoony, *Faith and Action* (Vallecito, CA: Ross House, 2019), 127.

strategies of subversion. By denying created reality as God-ordained, it reduces all material reality to evolutionary products of lesser worth.

When it infiltrated Christianity in the second century, Gnosticism therefore proceeded to identify the God of the Old Testament with the material world and the God of the New Testament with the spiritual. The old Gnostics also denied the humanity of Christ and his bodily resurrection, arguing that He was only a spirit. Material human beings—those occupied with physical realities such as food, clothing, family and money—were believed to be unable to be enlightened and achieve γνωστικός (*gnostikos*) or true knowledge.[2] In other words, to the Gnostics, all material things were inherently sinful. The profound implications of this heresy were recognized as such and consequently refuted by the likes of the church father Irenaeus, who beautifully polemicized against this heresy, by noting that their anti-materialism amounts to "despising the workmanship of God."[3]

Despite the successes of Irenaeus' polemics, the

2. Pheme Perkins, *Gnosticism and the New Testament* (Minneapolis, MN: Fortress Press, 1993), 45.

3. Irenaeus of Lyons, *Adversus Haeresus* (Cambridge: Typis academicis, 1857 [180]), I, 22, 1. This is my own translation of the Latin, which reads: "Plasma autem dei contemnunt." Irenaeus originally wrote in Greek and this work was originally (and aptly) entitled λεγχος καὶ ἀνατροπὴ τῆς ψευδωνύμου γνώσεως, which translates to "On the Detection and Overthrow of the So-Called Gnosis." However, as the original Greek text has been

heresy of Gnosticism has nonetheless remained with us and has reared its ugly head yet again in the modern church. As Rousas John Rushdoony remarks:

> We see today Gnosticism in the Church denying the physical resurrection of Jesus, six-day creation and much more. Creation is re-interpreted to mean evolution. God becomes a name for natural cause... Modern science, like philosophy and most churches, is gnostic. God cannot be the "first cause" (nor the last) because all causality is natural. The Bible cannot be a source of knowledge because all knowledge must be humanistic. Gnosticism in the twentieth century has captured virtually all seminaries and most churches. Its presuppositions are now basic to the pulpit.[4]

The implications of this Neo-Gnosticism are as immense as those of the old Gnosticism. Apart from the obvious fact that accepting gnostic doctrine and anthropology places us outside of salvation (1 John 4:3), it also has massive implications for the church's engagement in the world. Rushdoony explains this in what is perhaps one of the most profound theological statements ever written:

---

largely lost, the Latin translation which I used is the closest to a primary source in existence.

4. Rushdoony, *Faith and Action*, 396.

The Biblical faith concerning Jesus Christ involves and requires believing that He was raised from the dead in the same body which suffered crucifixion. Jesus Christ, by His resurrection, destroyed the power of sin and death. Moreover, He set forth His victory over the realms of both spirit and matter, conquering the enemy in every realm. If Jesus Christ had only risen from the dead as a spirit, as a ghost, then his only victory and his only saving power would be limited to the world of the spirit... It would mean that his people would be helpless against the powers of this world and without law and recourse in this world.

But, because Jesus Christ rose from the dead, He is Lord over all lords, King over all kings, the Lawgiver and supreme Governor of all things, material and spiritual... For this reason, from the days of the early church on, the Day of Resurrection has been a time of joy because it sets forth the certainty of victory in and through Jesus Christ...

We then, who are people of the resurrection, must live in the joy and the confidence of victory. This is our destiny, victory. Life is rarely easy, but with Christ our King, it is always good. We are generally in a battle, because the enemies are many, and the forces of evil real, but our victory has been assured and manifested by the resurrection of Jesus Christ.[5]

The implications of embracing Neo-Gnosticism have been truly devastating to the church's attempts at fulfilling its calling in the world. Liberal Theology's denial of the basic doctrines regarding creation, the virgin birth, and the bodily resurrection of Christ is, as Rushdoony notes, fundamentally rooted in Gnostic presuppositions, as is the rejection of the Lordship of Christ. Contrary to the biblical command to exercise dominion over all of creation by doing all things to the glory of God to the point of even taking every thought captive in obedience to Christ (Genesis 1:28; 1 Corinthians 10:31; 2 Corinthians 10:5), Gnosticism degrades all earthly realities and actions as inherently unholy. Through the heresy of Neo-Gnosticism, which by virtue of its rejection of creation also rejects the sovereignty of God as Creator, the Church has also succumbed to antinomianism, the heresy that rejects God's authority as Lawgiver and consequently His Law as ultimate moral standard.

But, you may ask at this point, what is the relationship between the anti-materialism of Neo-Gnosticism and the materialism of Marxism?

5. Rousas J. Rushdoony, *A Word in Season, Volume 2: Daily Messages on the Faith for all of Life* (Vallecito, CA: Ross House, 2011), 10.

Previously I explained how the materialist worldview of Marxism is the greatest contemporary threat to the church. Now I point to an anti-materialist theology in the church itself which has effectuated this takeover? Surely these two—Marxism and Gnosticism—are mutually exclusive? This might have been the case had it not been for the very dualistic worldview enabled by Gnosticism which is so prevalent in the church today. In an infusion of two antithetical ideologies, mainstream theologians have come to justify their agreement with Cultural Marxist egalitarianism based on a Neo-Gnostic premise, namely the supremacy of spiritual over physical realities. They then proceed to argue for the levelling of all social distinctions and social hierarchies as the inevitable result of this premise. This gross irrationalism has gone a long way in enabling Marxists to infiltrate and subvert our churches and seminaries. For example, because of this modernist theology's false Neo-Gnostic premise that spiritual realities trump physical realities, texts such as Galatians 3:28-29, which teaches that there is no spiritual distinction between men and women in Christ, can be abused to ally the Church with Cultural Marxist agendas such as feminism and transgenderism.

Furthermore, this dualistic alliance between Neo-Gnosticism and Cultural Marxism, based in their common premise of denying the sovereignty of God as Creator and Ruler of the universe, has in turn also paved the way for a second great heresy which has neutered the modern Church, namely Radical Two Kingdom Theology.

Radical Two Kingdom Theology

Radical Two Kingdom Theology (also known as "Reformed two kingdoms") is the heretical teaching that there are two distinct spheres in creation, the so-called spiritual and the so-called common or material realm, with Christ exercising authority through his Word only over the first of these—the spiritual realm. While advocates of this heresy also proclaim Christ's authority over the common realm, which includes everything from education and politics, to sports, socialization, sexuality, and work, they maintain that in this realm a natural law, which may or may not overlap with biblical law and in fact often contradicts the principles of biblical law, reigns supreme.[6] However, since the natural man, remaining unregenerated by the Holy Spirit, is depraved to the point being at enmity with God and his Law with all his thoughts and deeds (Romans 8:7), it should be quite obvious that the common ground sought with all unbelievers through natural law or common grace will always amount to antinomianism in practice. While we

---

6. David VanDrunen, *Natural Law and the Two Kingdoms: A Study in the Development of Reformed Social Thought* (Grand Rapids, MI: Eerdmans 2010), 306-307; Mark Larson, *Abraham Kuyper, Conservatism, and the Church and State.* (Eugene, OR: Wipf & Stock 2015), 16.

know that there is a natural revelation which goes out to all people without exception (Romans 1:20), this does not mean that unregenerate men receive this natural revelation without distorting it in the process. Nor does this imply that natural revelation alone is sufficient for the ordering, structuring, and directing of a healthy society. In fact, there are literally no examples of a sustainable and continually-advancing civilization outside of Christendom which has achieved the heights it has. The ones which have come the closest have perhaps been Japan and apostate Scandinavia after World War II. But with birthrates already under 1.5 children per woman and soaring national debts, neither of these examples come close to long-term sustainability.

Radical Two Kingdom theology is justified on liberal presuppositions—above all, the inherent goodness of mankind. Once you take the reality of human depravity and fallibility into account, there is simply no justification for a natural law—even if you acknowledge this to come from God— as functionally serving as a sufficient moral and legal framework providing the middle ground or common ground between Christians and unbelievers. The unregenerate may receive natural revelation in the same way those regenerated by the Holy Spirit do, but because of their hatred of God they will necessarily distort that revelation according to their godlessness (Jeremiah 17:9; Ephesians 2:1-3). Natural law can certainly be said to exist, and it is certainly useful in many circumstances.

However, natural law efficiently provides a good moral framework to unregenerate men only insofar as they remain inconsistent in their opposition to God. For example, the fact that natural law teaches us that a civilization that has fewer than two children per woman is going to die has not stopped the destructive rise of feminism in every First-World country on the globe, a satanic development which has effectuated exactly this suicidal fertility rate.

Another example: we know that lifelong monogamy is the natural and healthy state for both men and women—this is, after all, an integral part of God's created order (Genesis 2:24; Matthew 19:4-6). We also know, from research, such as that conducted which by the Oxford social anthropologist J.D. Unwin (1895—1936), that there is a direct and undeniable correlation between increased sexual liberation and socio-cultural decline.[7] The more promiscuous the women, the more ill-disciplined the men, the quicker the culture collapses and the quicker we lose all our nice things. This has been proven time and time again throughout history and is in line with the providential-covenantal decrees of a God Who is absolutely sovereign over creation. God has ordered creation in such a way that disobedience to his commandments, including his commandments relating to sexuality, always and inevitably leads to curses (Deuteronomy 28:15-

---

7. J.D. Unwin, *Sex and Culture* (London: Oxford, 1934), 1-4.

68). Sexual immorality and licentiousness are also expressly noted by the Apostle Paul as one of the most notable characteristics of a godless society under God's judgment (Romans 1:24-27).

As Christians living in the power and wisdom the Holy Spirit, we of course know this to be true. But try explaining this to the average secular young man or woman in apostate Western society—someone who has been indoctrinated by public school sex education and sexualized Hollywood movies all their lives. How would one go about using natural law to teach them these truths? How do you explain to them that fornication (having sex outside of the confines of the institution of marriage) is not only immoral, but actually bad for them as individuals, their families, and society as a whole? After all, they have been indoctrinated by the schools, the entertainment industry, and their peers that true manhood or womanhood is intrinsically related to an active sex life. How do you convince them that using birth control throughout most of their reproductive years is unhealthy to society as well as to themselves? Perhaps you could try to point them to scientific studies that have proven the negative impact of the use of hormonal contraception in terms of causing breast cancer.[8] Perhaps you could point them to the

---

8. Lina S. Mørch, Charlotte W. Skovlund, Philip C. Hannaford, Lisa Iversen, Shona Fielding, and Øjvind Lidegaard, "Contemporary Hormonal Contraception and the Risk of Breast Cancer," *New England Journal of Medicine* 377 (2017): 2230-2231.

long-term socio-economic impact of wasting your reproductive years on childless, hedonistic pleasure-seeking. You could try this, but if there has been one thing the response to the Covid-19 pandemic has taught is, it is that people rarely if ever believe scientific evidence as long as it is contradicted by a strong mass media narrative. This is because, as the Christian apologist Cornelius Van Til has pointed out, "revelation in nature was never meant to function by itself. It was from the beginning insufficient without its supernatural concomitant."[9] Therefore, without the enlightenment of the Holy Spirit, the sad reality is that most people are psychologically geared to believe whatever they are told to believe by those whom they (at times even subconsciously) perceive to be in authority. Their authority may be the mainstream media, the entertainment industry, or the government—but for the unregenerate it is never God. This reality also manifests in history. History has shown time and again that it is almost always a small minority of people in leadership positions and in positions of authority who have directed the course of society. As Rushdoony notes, "no era of history has ever been governed by majorities, but only by dedicated minorities who have provided the direction to others."[10]

---

9. Cornelius Van Til, "Nature and Scripture," in *The Infallible Word: A Symposium* (Philadelphia: Presbyterian Guardian Publishing, 1946), 259.

10. Rushdoony, *Faith and Action*, 206.

The fact that natural revelation can never properly function without the enlightenment of the Holy Spirit, has particular significance for the role of Christianity in general and biblical law in particular in the public domain. The entire idea behind Radical Two Kingdom theology is, after all, to accommodate unbelievers in a public domain which is supposedly ideologically neutral. However, society, law, politics, education, work, leisure, sports, and everything else that make up our human existence are never neutral but always and without exception driven and informed by a particular worldview. This public opinion and worldview are, for the most part, shaped by those in public authority. This also means that the public establishment of a particular religion is inevitable. All societies in all times have a public religion—this is an inescapable reality. If Christianity is not established as public religion, some other religion will fill the void. There is no neutrality. The claim of the post-World War II Western world to being a secular society, which supposedly entails an irreligious or post-religious public domain, could not be further removed from reality. It is not that the West has become any less religious than it had been in times past, but simply that the religion of the West has changed. This fact is now even recognized by leftist mainstream scholars such as the Georgetown University sociologist of religion José Casanova.[11] The national religion

---

11. José Casanova, *Global Religious and Secular*

of most Western countries has simply shifted from Christianity to Cultural Marxism.

When the neo-liberalism that had replaced communism as national religion in most Eastern European countries proved to be a massive failure during the 1990s, an ideological vacuum emerged in the public domain—one which in turn paved the way for the re-confessionalization of countries which today form the very heart of European Christendom, such as Hungary and Poland.

As Bavinck points out, the Radical Two Kingdom heresy effectuates a dualism between nature and grace which creates "such a sharp divide between the spiritual and the material, between the heavenly and the earthly, by which they are divided into two hemispheres and the relation between nature and grace or between creation and redemption is completely denied."[12]

In other words, all that the heresy of Radical Two Kingdom Theology does is destroy the positive impact of the gospel upon society and emasculate the church. It paves the way to victory for the enemies

Dynamics: The Modern System of Classification (Leiden: Brill, 2019), 22.

12. Herman Bavinck, *Gereformeerde dogmatiek, tweede deel* (Kampen: J.H. Bos, 1897), 534-535. This is my own translation of the original Dutch, which reads: "de scheiding tusschen het geestelijke en het wereldlijke, tusschen het hemelsche en het aardsche... zoo scherp doorgetrokken [wordt] en in twee hemisphaeria ingedeeld, dat het verband van natuur en genade, van schepping en herschepping geheel wordt miskend."

of Christ who seek to overthrow all that reminds them of Christendom. The main reason that Radical Two Kingdom theologians always fail at creating common ground with the so-called "secular world" is because of that world's hatred of Christian civilization. And why do they hate Christian civilization? Because it reminds them of Christ, and they hate Him. When Jesus said that anyone who is not with Him is against Him, our Savior clearly implied that there is no neutrality in any sphere of life (Matthew 12:30; Luke 11:23). Whether we engage in private activities at home or in social activities, whether we are at work or school or dining out, we are to always do everything in obedience to God, in accordance with His Law, and to his glory (1 Corinthians 10:31). The Lordship of Christ over every aspect of creation renders Radical Two Kingdom Theology both heretical and impotent.

All of Life Redeemed

Both Neo-Gnosticism and Radical Two Kingdom Theology infringe upon the crown rights of our Lord Jesus Christ. The Dutch Calvinist theologian Abraham Kuyper famously (and rightly) stated that all people and all nations are called to obey Christ in all that we do, since there is not a single square inch of all reality over which Christ is not Sovereign King in the absolute sense.[13]

---

13. Abraham Kuyper, *Souvereiniteit in eigen kring*

This extends to all human activity and knowledge. When dealing with morality this is quite evident, but what often remains unrecognized, is that Christ's Lordship extends even to the most exact sciences. For example, one can and should even distinguish a Christian from a non-Christian mathematics. Ancient pre-Christian mathematicians showed a distinct aversion to the idea of infinity. Aristotle, for example, regarded actual infinity to be a mathematical impossibility. Christians, however, do not share this aversion to infinity, because we know that Christ, the Logos, is infinite. It was therefore a Christian mathematician George Cantor (1845–1918), who developed *set theory*, which is now widely regarded as a central principle of mathematics, in which he showed the importance of one-to-one correspondence between the members of two sets, defined infinite and well-ordered sets, and proved that the real numbers are more numerous than natural numbers. In fact, Cantor's theory implies the existence of an infinity of infinities. Cantor intrinsically linked his mathematical breakthrough to its philosophical and theological implications—he identified the Absolute Infinite with God, and he considered his work on transfinite numbers to have been revealed to him by God, Who had providentially decreed him to be the person to reveal it to the world.[14]

(Amsterdam: Kruyt, 1880), 32.

14. Anthony Patton, *The End of Infinity: Where Math-*

With Christ as Logos and Absolute Infinite Creator of mathematics, Christians have traditionally viewed mathematics as a subset of Logic, but many modern anti-Christian mathematicians during the twentieth and twenty-first centuries have forsaken this traditional Logicist view in favor of what has become known as the Formalist view of mathematics, which is again characterized by a return to finitism (i.e. the denial of infinity). This bizarre theory is upheld by contemporary mathematicians such as Shaughan Lavine from the University of Arizona and Jean Paul van Bendegem from the Free University of Brussels in Belgium.[15]

Science itself, as the interpretation of divine thought as manifested in divine works, is fundamentally based on the conviction that the universe is the product of a divine reason or logic. Modern science's endless search for causes can be attributed to the widespread forsaking of the belief in the existence of a rational order and consistent logic operating in creation—an order and logic which can only be the design of a Sovereign Creator.[16] True science should always lead to increased knowledge and reverence for God. The Christian philosophy

---

ematics and Philosophy Meet (New York: Algora), 3.

15. Jean Paul van Bendegem, "A Defense of Strict Finitism," *Constructivist Foundations* 7 (2012):141-149.

16. Stanley Jaki, *The Origin of Science and the Science of Its Origin* (Edinburgh: Scottish Academic Press, 1979), 2.

of science is unmissable for solid scientific scholarship given the reality of human nature itself.
Since human beings are morally depraved, humans
exhibit a tendency to distort truth for the sake of
self-interest. Only the self-evaluation demanded by
the gospel of Jesus Christ can keep us on the path to
finding scientific truth. It is therefore categorically
false to speak of any kind of "objective science"
as if scientific research could ever proceed in a
vacuum without set pre-investigative presuppositions—something increasingly recognized by even
leading bon-Christian scholars today.[17] This does
not mean we cannot distinguish between true and
false science, however. True science is necessarily
Christocentric, since it is only through Jesus Christ
that all objects of scientific study as well as the
study of creation itself find meaning and purpose.

Christ is not only the Origin and End of all being
(Romans 11:36), but He is also the foundation of
all knowledge itself (Acts 17:28). Facts, therefore,
find their meaning and coherence within the inescapable framework provided by God's sovereign
providence over and plan for Creation as manifested
in the history of the world. Facts are therefore never
merely theoretical abstractions to be understood in
isolation from practical reality, but facts are always
manifested through their revelation as providen-

---

17. Lisa Osbeck, "We still aren't Certain what we're
Doing: Reflections on the Complexities of Psychological
Science and Intersubjective Epistemology," *Journal of
Constructivist Psychology* 33(1), 2020: 43.

tially ordained realities in inescapable relation to their origin in God as Creator and their ultimate fulfillment in the divine purpose of creation: the glorification of Christ as Lord.

Forsaking the authority of God in any sphere of life therefore has dire and inescapable consequences. It is in light of this reality that our calling to take every single human thought captive in obedience to Christ should be understood (2 Corinthians 10:5). Sadly, the church has for the most part forsaken the truth of Christ's absolute Lordship over all spheres of life, as well as the practical calling it entails. For the sake of comfort, for the sake of avoiding conflict, or as a result of downright apostasy, churches have chosen to withdraw from the difficult and often complex realities of the modern world instead choosing to isolate itself in a kind of spiritual retreat from the world. This is because both Neo-Gnosticism and Radical Two Kingdom Theology is fundamentally antinomian, and antinomianism (the heresy that rejects God's authority as absolute Lawgiver) is inherently defeatist and retreatist. Rushdoony aptly describes the weakness and loser-mentality of antinomians as follows:

> They fail to see the relevance of God's Law as the way of sanctification and as the law of men and nations. They do not recognize God's law as God's plan for dominion, for godly authority and rule in every area of life. This anti-law attitude guarantees impo-

tence and defeat to all churches who hold to it. They may prosper as convents or retreats from the world, but never as a conquering army of God.[18]

We have not lost the culture war because there is an inherent strength in the forces of darkness able to overpower the church militant. We have lost the culture war because we have not fought as Christian soldiers are called to do (1 Samuel 17:45). We have surrendered in the name of tolerance, peace, and acceptance instead of fighting vigorously and passionately in the most Holy Name of our Lord Jesus Christ.

18. Rousas John Rushdoony, *God's Plan for Victory: The Meaning of Postmillennialism* (Vallecito, CA: Ross House, 1977), 77.

CHAPTER 5

A Declaration of War: Our Calling and Duty as the Church Militant

THE PACIFISM OF the contemporary church is completely unacceptable. It amounts to nothing less than cowardly disobedience to Christ. And the Bible has no nice things to say about cowards. Revelation 21 describes the new heaven and earth where children of God enjoy His glory for eternity. The text proceeds to inform us that only those who overcome the temptation and sin of the world—the children of God—will inherit the glories and pleasures of this eternal paradise (Revelation 21:8). Those who succumbed to sin will not be received into glory but will be thrown in the eternal lake of fire and brimstone (Revelation 21:8b). However, in writing Revelation 21:8 the Holy Spirit also inspired the apostle to expressly mention a number of sinners who will inherit this eternal torment: the cowardly, the unbelievers, those who practice abominations, murderers, those who practice sexual immorality, sorcerers, idolators, and liars. The first category included in this list of the reprobate are the cowardly, as the Greek word δειλοῖς (*deilois*) is commonly translated. The word literally refers to cowards, that is those who are driven by fear or those for whom fear is the decisive factor in their actions. In other words, fear itself is not the sin, but rather the refusal to act in accordance with God's command and calling because our fear of someone or something else trumps our fear of God. This is exactly what the Church's reluctance to engage in the culture war amounts to. But to those who fear men more than God, God eventually reveals His superior power and glory by casting them into the lake of fire, a far more terrifying punishment than any human or demon whom they had feared could ever inflict upon them. The implications of Revelation 21:8 is clear—if we are too cowardly to stand up and fight for the crown rights of the King of kings in the public domain, then that very King will judge and punish us severely and eternally.

But Isn't Our Battle "Not Against Flesh and Blood"?

One favorite verse the neo-Gnostics and Radical Two Kingdom theologians love to abuse is Ephesians 6:12, which reads "For we do not wrestle against flesh and blood, but against principalities, against powers, against the rulers of the darkness of this age, against spiritual hosts of wickedness in the heavenly places" (Ephesians 6:12). This verse, also often invoked in defense of some form of pacifism, is abused to justify an escapist theology reducing the physical world, the world we experience and live in every moment of our earthly lives, to being irrelevant for the kingdom of God, whereas "spiritual" things such as prayer, worship services, and Bible study are proposed as being the true realm of religious exercise. This amounts to a dualist conception of the world based in the Neo-Gnosticism treated in the previous chapter— with the proposition being that physical realities are somehow inferior to spiritual realities. But the spiritual always affects and shapes the physical. Denying this amounts to a complete disregard for biblical social ontology,[1] in which the central function of grace is not to liberate us from creation and nature, but to redeem nature itself. As the Dutch theologian Herman Bavinck aptly describes it:

God does not manifest his covenant of grace by ripping people away from their humanity and establishing a covenantal community outside of our natural state, but he brings that covenant into humanity itself, makes it part of the world, and ensures that it remains protected from evil in the world. As Redeemer, God follows the

1. Social Ontology is that branch of Philosophy which studies the nature, structure, and properties of the social world of human interaction and existence.

same path He does as Creator and Ruler of all things. Grace is something different to nature, but it joins with nature so as not to destroy it but rather to renew it. Grace is not an inheritance that is not acquired by virtue of natural descent, but it is covenantally maintained through the natural relations embedded in human nature. The covenant of grace does not randomly jump to and from one individual to the next, but is maintained through families, generations and nations in an organic fashion.[2]

Denying divinely ordained and created realities

---

2. Herman Bavinck, *Handleiding bij het onderwijs in den Christelijke godsdienst* (Kampen: Kok), 115-116. This is my own translation of the original Dutch, which reads: "God verwezenlijkt zijn genadeverbond niet, door op den tast eenige menschen uit de menschheid uit te lezen en dan buiten de wereld om saam te voegen; maar Hij draagt het in de menschheid in, maakt het tot een bestanddeel der wereld, en zorgt nu, dat het in die wereld bewaard blijve van den booze. Als Herschepper wandelt Hij in het spoor, dat Hij als Schepper, Onderhouder en Regeerder aller dingen getrokken heeft. De genade is iets anders en hoogers dan de natuur, maar zij sluit zich toch bij de natuur aan, en vernietigt ze niet doch herstelt ze. Zij is geen erfgoed, dat krachtens natuurlijke geboorte overgaat, maar ze stroomt toch voort in de bedding, welke in de natuurlijke verhoudingen van het menschelijk geslacht is uitgegraven. Het verbond der genade springt niet van den hak op den tak, maar zet in de familiën, geslachten en volken op eene historische en organische wijze zich voort."

amounts to an epistemic shift away from the recognition of the sovereignty of God as Creator and providential Ruler to elevating a man-made social order over that which has been ordained by God. The impact of this heresy can be seen even in the theology of so-called "conservative" theologians, such as the holder of the John Gresham Machen chair as professor of theology at Westminster Seminary California, Michael Horton. For example, Horton writes that "there is no such thing as a Christian nation other than the body of Christ, which admits no distinctions of race, culture, class or sex before God."[3] Pretending that the biological realities and the hard facts of everyday life are irrelevant to the gospel does not make it so. As human beings we are fully dependent creatures designed by a sovereign and independent God who governs creation for his purposes. Ignoring the divinely-created realities of nature, such as differences in sex, ethnicity, and race, as well as all other distinct identities created by God, is a form of humanism, that is, an attempt to remake reality in your own image as opposed to submitting to the authority and sovereignty of God and His wisdom as *pantokrator* or ruler of all things (2 Corinthians 6:18; Revelation 1:8).

Compare the liberal stance of Horton with the historical interpretation of texts such as Galatians

3. Michael Horton, *Putting Amazing Back Into Grace: Embracing the Heart of the Gospel* (Grand Rapids, MI: Baker Books, 2011), 23.

3:28-29, which teaches that there is no distinction or preference *with regard to the unmerited salvation we receive in Christ* before God. Prior to the advent of modern Liberalism and Cultural Marxism this passage was not historically understood as making a claim regarding social ontology, as is confirmed by the church father Augustine's interpretation of this passage:

> Differences with regard to race (*gentium*), condition (*conditiones*) and sex (*sexus*)... remain imbedded in human interactions, and the apostles themselves teach that they are to be respected throughout the course of life. They even proposed living in accordance with the racial differences (*differentia gentis)* between Jews and Greeks as a wholesome rule.[4]

The same apostle Paul who wrote that there is no distinction between male and female in Christ, under the guidance of the Holy Spirit, limited the office of pastor to men only (1 Corinthians 14:34-35 and 1 Timothy 2:11-14). By simply employing

---

4. Aurelius Augustine, *Opera Omnia, tomus tertius, pars altera* (Paris: Gallice, 1841), 2125. This is my own translation of the original Latin, which reads "differentia ista vel gentium, vel conditiones, vel sexus... manet in conversatione mortali; eiusque ordinem in huius vitae itinere servandum esse, et Apostoli praecipunt, qui etiam regulas saluberrimas tradunt, quemadmodum secum vivant pro differentia gentis Judaei en Graeci."

the orthodox hermeneutical principle of *analogia fidei* ("analogy of faith"), i.e. that Scripture is to be interpreted by the Holy Spirit speaking through Scripture itself, it becomes clear that the traditional interpretation of texts such as Galatians 3:28-29, as embodied by Augustine, is the orthodox one.

In other words, while God is no respecter of persons and does not show favoritism (Acts 10:34-35), this does not imply that the physical world in all of its manifestations is not to be cultivated and sanctified to His glory. Our families, nations, and cultures matter to God, Who is the sovereign Creator thereof, and these realities are to be sanctified by the gospel (Matthew 28:19).

Understanding the importance of God-given realities in creation and in the kingdom of God is also central to rightly understanding passages such as Ephesians 6:12, which teaches that our battle is not against flesh and blood but against spiritual powers. As Christians, we are part of a spiritual kingdom, and the enemies of that kingdom fight a spiritual war against this kingdom. But this does not preclude the enemy from using physical (flesh-and-blood) means in this war. After all, this spiritual kingdom we are part of consist of individuals, families, and nations. And the fact that the forces of darkness are waging a spiritual war, does not preclude battling on the physical front against us as individuals, families, and nations as part of their warfare strategy against the kingdom of God. In fact, the fact that our enemies fight a spiritual battle does not even make the battle we as Christians engage in that distinct from the way in which war has always generally been conceived by military theorists. The famous ancient Chinese military theorist, Sun Tzu, in fact, emphasized the spiritual nature of military conflict in his famous work *The Art of War* when he wrote that "to subdue the enemy without fighting is the supreme excellence."[5] War is always hybrid. It is always both psychological and spiritual in addition to being physical. The same is true for the battle we wage for the kingdom of God. While the battle is primarily fought on a spiritual front, it most certainly has physical manifestations.

These physical manifestations of the war against the forces of Satan include physical warfare, political warfare, social warfare, information warfare, and cultural warfare. We, the followers of Christ here on earth, are called the Church Militant precisely because we, in contradistinction to the believers already in heaven (the Church Triumphant), are engaging in a war against the forces of darkness here on earth, that is, in the context of the physical, created reality we find ourselves in. We are at war, and if there is one thing I hope the reader has seen evidenced in this book so far is that this war encompasses every facet of life—it pertains to us as individuals, to us as families, to us

5. Sun-tzu, *The Art of War*, trans. Y. Shibing, (Kent: Woodsworth, 1998), 25.

as communities, to us as nations, to the workplace, to our social life, and to every activity we engage in. Christ, our King, is Lord over all, and we are to fight for his Lordship everywhere we go and in everything we do. Onwards, Christian soldiers!

The Church's Strategic Military Position at the Gates of Hell

In Old Testament times, Mount Hermon, the southern tip of the Anti-Lebanon mountain range, was considered to be the dwelling place of idols and demons (Judges 3:3, 1 Chronicles 5:23). Because the mountain is the place where demons live (Psalm 68:22), the base of mount Hermon characterized by its deep ravines, came to be known as "the gates of hell."[6] During New Testament times, the town Caesarea Philippi built at the feet of Mount Hermon was also widely known for its commitment to idolatry—especially the cult of the Greek god Pan—as well as its degenerate culture,[7] thereby confirming the association with hell or hades in the minds of the Jewish people.

In Matthew 16, Jesus is in Magdala in Galilee. But He takes his disciples all the way to Syria—50

---

6. This fact was brought to my attention by Dr. Michiel Durand, a Pretoria-based general surgeon, philosopher, and Hebrew scholar during a personal visit at his home.

7. Raymond Culpepper and Floyd Carey, *No Church Left behind: Every Church can be Great* (Cleveland, TN: Pathway Press), 32.

miles to the north, to Mount Hermon, to the very gates of hell, to ask of them a simple question: "Who do you say I am?" (Matthew 16:15). And when Peter answers that He is the Christ, the Son of the living God, Jesus says: "You are Peter. And upon this rock," that is, this very rock upon which they were standing, this very rock right in front of the gates of hell—not far away and secluded in Jerusalem, but upon this very rock right here, "I will build my church" (Matthew 16:18). And what will the church be doing at the gates of hell? Engaging in warfare and besieging those gates: militantly conquering, overthrowing, and crushing the kingdom of Satan—not only Jerusalem, not only Judea and Samaria, not only the world, but the very gates of hell, for Christ our King. And in encouraging us to victory in this greatest of battles—a battle where we are not merely defending our territory (in Jerusalem), but attacking the very gates of hell (in Hermon)—He triumphantly proclaims: "The gates of hell shall not prevail against it" (Matthew 16:18).

Roman Catholics historically understood the "rock" upon which Christ builds His church to be the person of Peter. Protestants have historically understood it to mean Peter's confession. I believe that it is neither. Understanding the immediate geography of where the scene took place is key to understanding the significance of the passage. As the contemporary Old Testament scholar and geographer, Barry J. Beitzel points out:

In light of the massive rock scarp against which Caesarea Philippi was built and into which were hewn images of dead gods and goddesses, Jesus may have been using *petra* to refer to the worldviews represented in that rock face. They appeared to be insurmountable but, here, Jesus was declared to be the Living God. In other words, this encounter represented a stinging condemnation of all forms of pagan worship.[8]

Caesarea Philippi was built upon a rock which symbolized the philosophical and religious foundation upon which the people of that city's lives—characterized by idolatry and sin—were built. Over against and in contradistinction to this worldly culture, Christ proclaims a new way of life and its superiority over worldliness. Rather than referring to the person of Peter or his confession, the rock upon which Christ proclaims He will build His Church therefore refers to *the military positioning and calling of Christ's church on earth*. In other words, what Jesus is doing here is giving us, His Church Militant, the orders for the battle. We are to position ourselves at the gates of hell because we are on the attack. We are not to be merely defending and trying to preserve those small bastions of the faith which Cultural Marxism has

8. Barry Beitzel, *Lexham Geographic Commentary on the Gospels*, "Peter's Declaration at Caesarea Philippi," (Bellingham, WA: Lexham Press, 2016).

not yet destroyed, subverted, and infiltrated. But we are to exercise dominion aggressively and militantly. We are to dismantle the very foundations of all worldviews which rebel against the sovereign Lordship of Christ our King. Once we have made gains, we are also called to capitalize upon those gains as a relentless army dedicated to one goal: the expansion of God's Kingdom on earth. The City of Man needs to be crushed so that the very rock upon which it was built can be reclaimed to serve as foundation for the City of God. The church father Augustine therefore describes the nature and calling of the flock of Christ in his famous work on *The City of God* as "that kingdom militant, in still maintaining conflict with the enemy, and waging war with warring lusts, is laying government upon them as they yield, until we come to that most peaceful kingdom in which we shall reign without an enemy."[9] We are to wage war upon the enemies of Christ and crush them wherever we may find them. They must be destroyed by the army of the risen King, for He has already conquered every enemy and is, partially through us as vessels, subduing all enemies under His feet (1 Corinthians 15:25) and crushing their heads (Genesis 3:15).

---

9. Aurelius Augustine, *De Civitate Dei* (Turnhout, Belgium: Brepols Publishers, 2003), Liber XX, IX. "regno militiae, in quo adhuc cum hoste confligitur et aliquando repugnatur pugnantibus uitiis, aliquando cedentibus imperatur, donec ueniatur ad illud pacatissimum regnum, ubi sine hoste regnabitur."

Over the past several decades, the Left has been actively waging war against Christianity. They have infiltrated and subverted all our institutions from the inside out, thereby destroying the remnants of Christendom in the West. In the process we have not only lost almost all of the battles, but also lost immense ground in the war because we have become passive as our theology has become passive. There is far too little active resistance, indeed, too little militant resistance against the forces of darkness seeking to destroy us because they hate Christ our King. We are weakened and out of position. We are scattered and confused. This cannot be allowed to continue. We must set up our forces at the gates of hell according to our King's orders and fight with our very lives to conquer and crush those gates. We must launch a militant resistance and a relentless attack on all fronts. Above all else, we are called to advance a kingdom.

But What Are We to Do Now?

All of this might sound good in theory. Attack! Siege! Conquer! But what does this mean in practice? We are undoubtedly on the backfoot. We are disorganized and have no institutions or structures to serve as solid foundations from where to launch any effective attack against the enemies of Christ, never mind annihilate them. So what then should be our *modus operandi*?

In the first few chapters of this book, I emphasized the central role of moral, political, and religious subversion in the strategies employed by the Left in their efforts to destroy Christianity, and as such I believe this should be the first front on which our resistance ought to focus. We ought to militantly oppose and fight the moral subversion brought about by the Left over the past several decades. But we are to do so using wise, resolute and effective strategies. Given the nature of the current predicament we find ourselves in, we are, in order to accomplish our eventual goals, to start the battle at home.

First, make sure to do family Bible study every day. Turn off those godless programs on television. Stop supporting corporations that hate you and hate Jesus Christ. Stop buying their products. Be as self-sufficient as you possibly can. Buy land and books. If you can escape the labor market and start your own viable business, do so. If you cannot start your own business, try to find employment at a local business as opposed to working for a large corporation which work against the interests of the kingdom of Christ. Be active on social media. With new dissident and Christian platforms being added regularly, there should, God willing, be ample (and increasing) opportunities for us to advance the kingdom of Christ through social media use in future—despite the current censorship measures employed by Big Tech. Through social media, our reach has been expanded tremendously. Social media needs to be valued as a gift from God to be employed to counter false mainstream media narratives. If there is a conservative church in the area, attend weekly worship services with your family. If not, start a home church and perhaps even invite like-minded people in your area to join you for worship. Sadly, because of the successes of Cultural Marxists in terms of infiltrating the church, some God-fearing families nowadays opt out of joining a local church and attending weekly services. While I sympathize with those who avoid going to church because so many churches serve a Leftist agenda, I am not convinced that this is a wise course of action, especially not in the long run. If there is legitimately no church in your area where the Gospel of Jesus Christ is preached and the sacraments rightly administered, then one really has the obligation to start such a church. The Belgic Confession of Faith teaches in article 28 that

> no person of whatsoever state or condition he may be, ought to withdraw himself, to live in a separate state from [the true Church]; but that all men are in duty bound to join and unite themselves with it; maintaining the unity of the Church; submitting themselves to the doctrine and discipline thereof.

Christendom cannot be rebuilt without the central institution around which the life of our communities are to revolve and by which they are to be sanctified: the local congregation. This does not mean, of course, that one should ever join a false church just for the sake of being part of a local congregation. It must always be remembered that the church is made up of sinful individuals and will never be perfect here on earth. We must also remember that submitting to the discipline of church officers does not entail that they have the right to infringe upon the authority fathers as the heads of their households have within the sphere of the family, the most basic unit of human society. The family precedes all other spheres of society within the covenantal social order established by God. But the precedence of the family over the church does not mean that the church is less necessary to a flourishing covenantal social order which glorifies God. In my own personal experience I have seen time and again how children from conservative households who do not attend worship services regularly, apostatize from the faith. This of course, does not mean that attending church is in and of itself a guarantee that your children will persevere in the faith. To the contrary, attending a false church in any Western nation today almost guarantees turning them into Leftists. But the fact of the matter is that the God-fearing local church is just as essential to a healthy Christian social order as God-fearing families.

Thankfully, more and more true churches are springing up all around the globe. Oftentimes these are house churches in rural areas consisting of only 3-5 families, but as insignificant as this may seem, this is an essential primary step in our battle against the forces of darkness. Moreover, isolation is one of the central means by which our enemies seek to conquer and defeat us. Since the Enlightenment, the Left's strategy has been one of divide and conquer, deliberately breaking down relationships, trust and social cohesion in the family, the church and in nations themselves. Unity must never be sought at the cost of truth, but at the same time we must not fall into the trap of giving Christ's enemies exactly what they want. It is precisely because local Christian community life has been so aggressively disrupted, that we currently lack even lesser magistrates as God-given line of defense against government tyranny.[10]

Arm yourself. Physically and mentally prepare yourself to reach the point where you would be willing to use violence to defend your property and your family against criminals and domestic terrorists. Educate your loved ones in the basic rules of firearm safety. It might also be a good idea to learn some form of martial arts for the purpose of self-defense. The time when we could simply

---

10. For a proper and thorough overview of the Christian doctrine of the lesser magistrate and the duty of Christian magistrates to resist government tyranny, see Wisconsin-based pastor Matt Trewhella's book *The Doctrine of the Lesser Magistrates: A Proper Resistance to Tyranny and a Repudiation of Unlimited Obedience to Civil Government* (Scotts Valley, CA: CreateSpace Independent Publishing Platform, 2013).

rely upon police forces to defend our lives and property, is long gone. Exceptions notwithstanding, police forces around the world have time and again shown themselves willing to side with the governments who pay their salaries, even against the cause of justice. Furthermore, growing up and living in a country where my people are consistently being targeted by terrorist mobs has taught me that the only armed response consistently able to avert attacks on you home and family and save lives, is your own and maybe that of a trustworthy neighbor.

Become active in your local community. Regardless of whether you are living in an urban or rural area, it is important that your community take responsibility for your local public services (infrastructure, education, water supply, waste management, etc.), your local security and defense, welfare, and socio-political life. The rise of tyranny is largely a result of our failure as families and communities to take responsibility for our own affairs. Resisting tyranny requires a paradigm shift in terms of our socio-political thinking. We ultimately need to do away with the current over-emphasis on "human rights" and move towards an increased and revitalized appraisal of the duties and responsibilities each of us have towards God and our neighbor. As Rushdoony points out:

> In any society, great or small, as the measure
> of coercion increases, the sense of respon-

sibility diminishes. As men find themselves able to surrender authority to the state, church or school, both their irresponsibility increases, and their complaints. Very often, in authoritarian regimes, cynical humor, complaining and bickering are irresponsible man's only way of asserting his superiority to foolish authorities without assuming any share of responsibility for himself. Such cynicism and complaining exists, not as true protest, but as a form of compliance. It is not a sign of health, but of radical sickness.[11]

Support local businesses, especially Christian businesses. Start a local Bible study in your neighborhood. Help organize or at least attend local cultural and social events. Help organize and participate in community projects, such as caring for the poor and handicapped, assisting at the local animal shelter, and cleaning up your streets and parks. Our reliance upon government, particularly a godless government, to do all these things for us is a central reason why we have become so helpless and weak. The same goes for our reliance upon Hollywood for our entertainment. Get involved with a local community radio station, or start a community podcast or group on social media. Run a community library, which can even be done on various social media platforms nowadays. Identify the local social

---

11. Rushdoony, *Intellectual Schizophrenia*, 131.

hotspots where people get together for social events in your community, and start building personal relationships with those who live in your vicinity. In this way you will not only have the opportunity to meet like-minded people and build healthy and God-honoring relationships, but you can also contribute to keeping the community engaged with each other and establish social cohesion.

If you have children whom you homeschool, try to connect with like-minded homeschooling families in your neighborhood and organize fun and educational outings for the children. If you are young and single, reach out to other believers in your community and help organize fun events like dances and barbecues. Go out to a local pub with a few close friends and enjoy some drinks. Avoid impersonal and urban night clubs. Local pubs and bars should be a place of familiar faces where the local community can get together for a fun time, while avoiding the degeneracy that so often characterizes urban nightlife. Intergenerational pubs and social or sports clubs are certainly a more wholesome social environment for young people to relax after a hard week's work than the currently prevalent and exclusively peer-orientated urban nightlife.

We also need to move away from college campus culture completely. That young people in the prime of their lives leave their own families and communities to go live in fraternities or apartments where they interact only with their peers is one of the most destructive aspects of modern life in this Cultural

Marxist social order, and it is fertile ground for sexual immorality and other forms of degeneracy. Campus life itself cultivates liberalism. As students are isolated from their families, communities, and cut off from their roots they absorb this campus life and become liberals. The campus becomes the student's new community, but it is a temporary one he is destined to leave behind after only a few short years. The very experience of campus life—which has become a vacation from reality—teaches the student to think of human beings as replaceable. Thanks to technological advances, college campuses have largely become outdated and superfluous. It is possible to get any number academic qualifications completely online. Even many trade schools could function largely online if there are community businesses willing to take on apprentices for practical experiences. There are also a large number of very practical benefits to taking education online including increased flexibility, which allows students to gain much-needed work experience while studying, being more cost-effective for both the university as well as the student's family, and ensuring greater access to wider variety of tailor-made programs. There is simply no reason for ambitious and talented young people in this day and age to leave and become isolated from their communities. Even highly skilled young people who cannot find employment with a local business could still potentially work remotely for larger companies from home. Countering the prevalent practice and culture of young people leaving communities would also help communities be what they by divine design were always supposed to be: clans, tribes, or extended families.

A central aspect of community involvement entails working together with leaders in your neighborhood to organize an emergency defense plan and make sure everyone in the community is on board with it. Ask your neighbors if they would be willing to help you defend your property and family against domestic terrorism and, God forbid, even government tyranny, if the time comes. Assure them that you would be willing to do the same for them. Encourage your community to arm them-selves, and encourage the men in your community to stay physically fit. If you are called to it, run for local office on an explicitly Christian and the-onomic[12] platform. Even if you are not called to

---

12. Theonomy, from the Greek Θεός ("Theos") meaning God and νόμος ("Nomos") meaning Law, is the principle that the ethics of biblical law is normative for all societies in all times and contexts. The term itself designates what has historically commonly been referred to as theocracy and originated within the context of the Counter-Enlightenment. The Enlightenment had effec-tuated what the University of North Texas sociologist Milan Zafirovsky describes as "a profound discontinu-ity, even direct or indirect revolutionary break, from Christian theocracy and civilization" (Zafirovsky, *The Enlightenment and its Effects on Modern Society* [New York: Springer, 2010], 93-94). Thomas Paine (1737–1809), the American Enlightenment philosopher, for example, acknowledged that the Enlightenment-based revolution in the system of government as it manifested

political office, engage in local community activism aimed at ridding your community from degenerate filth such as prostitution, swinger communities, and abortion mills. Once your family-life is in order,

---

in France and would later manifest all over the Western world, was intrinsically connected to "a revolution in the system of religion," arguing that any connection between religion and politics is an "adulterous" one, and adding that the political implications of Enlightenment epistemics are intrinsically dependent upon a complete revolution in the system of religion (Thomas Paine, *The Writings of Thomas Paine* [New York: Putnam, 1896], 22). The nineteenth-century British historian, sir Henry James Sumner Maine (1822–1888), utilized this same Enlightenment notion of political liberation from religion to propose a historical narrative in which pre-modern societies supposedly functioned within the legal framework of the "rule of religion" as opposed to the "rule of law" (Henry Sumner Maine, *Ancient Law: Its Connection with the Early History of Society and its Relation to Modern Ideas* [London: John Murray, 1861], 22).

However, this dichotomy would be challenged, perhaps most notably, by the influential Neo-Calvinist theologian, Herman Bavinck (1854–1921), who argued that "man is never autonomous, but always and everywhere bound to laws not conceived of by himself, but prescribed unto him by God as rule for his life," and that therefore any notions of autonomy amount to self-deception because of the inescapability of a moral framework for human existence, arguing for "theonomy" as the only alternative to false notions of autonomy and the only moral framework that does not descend into chaos and anarchy, and that "gives unto any creature its rightful place and its true meaning" (My own translation from Bavinck's *Christelijke Wereldbeschouwing* [Kampen: Kok, 1913], 101-102). The term itself, as far as I have been able to establish, therefore originated with Bavinck.

your community should be your second priority. It might at times seem counter-intuitive in the context of our globalized and atomized social order to take the step to reach out to your neighbors and request them to become actively involved in community life, but this is only because our society has already been destroyed by Cultural Marxism. Living in complete isolation from your community is both counterproductive and certainly not glorifying to God. If we are going to stand any chance of bringing down this godless new world order, we must start by reforming our own communities.

There may be a few obstacles to becoming involved with your local community, which is worth addressing here. First, if you live in a multi-cultural or heterogeneous community, this greatly impairs the potential for social cohesion. In such a case it would be best to try and move into or at least nearby a community that is homogeneous and preferably rural. If you cannot do so, cooperation with others in your heterogeneous community could be very complicated, but try to at least get others on board in terms of security and emergency plans. Second, it may be that your community is largely non-Christian or only nominally Christian. In such a case, evangelism enters into the equation as a top priority. You can still work together with the pagans in your community on security and defense plans or provide basic services to the community through projects to help the poor and the vulnerable or clean up the environment. But living in a Christian community is a prerequisite when it comes to cooperation with that community on matters such as the education of children, establishing local media, and organizing social or cultural events. Again, the ideal framework for enabling constructive community involvement and action is when that community is both Christian and homogeneous. This is the kind of community we need to aspire to live in and the kind of community we are called to transform to the glory of God. Third, it may be that a few of the leadership figures in your community are simply difficult people who are not easy to work with. If they refuse to get on board with the community programs, it is best to shake the dust from your feet and put in the extra effort to find people who would be cooperative. Take the lead yourself if need be.

On a national level, we as believers also have a particular calling. Like the prophets of the Old Testament, we as New Testament believers are also called to be prophetic voices in admonishing and exhorting others (Colossians 3:16; Hebrews 3:13). Jesus Himself has called us to evangelize the nations and to prioritize our own nation in this process (Matthew 19:28; Acts 1:8; 1 Timothy 5:8). God has placed us in a particular country and in a particular ethnic group for a reason, and we have been endowed with certain duties towards our own people. God expects us to call our own people to repentance and to prioritize them in our evangelism efforts so that nations can be Christianized and God can be glorified (Acts 17:26-27). After all, nations—having a much broader reach, influence, and longer lifespan than the individuals, families, and churches that make up a nation—are also uniquely equipped to advance the kingdom of God in the world in a way that individuals, families, and churches could never do. Christian nations can run a national Christian media and punish evil with the sword, thereby creating a suitable environment for intergenerational covenantal Christianity to flourish in the lives of families and in the public life over generations. Christian nations can defend the faith against attacks from globalists and bear a spectacular witness for Christ on international political platforms and on the global sports scene for the whole world to see in a way that individuals, local churches, and families never could. However, since there are virtually no Christian nations currently on earth, with perhaps the possible exception of a couple of Central and Eastern European nations, it means that for most of us, our current focus and priority should be our families and communities.

In other words, starting at home, proceeding to the extended family and community and finally the nation, should be our counterstrategy against the leftist forces waging war upon us as representatives of Christ our King.

It is vital to engage in this battle with the right perspective and mindset, without which we will never be able to constructively engage in this fight. One of the ways in which the modern world has managed to pollute our thinking and neutralize the church in the culture war, has been by virtue of convincing the church to, in syncretistic fashion, incorporate the secularization thesis into its eschatology. In doing so, the church has largely adopted an eschatological pessimism with its expectation of increased secularization which has, on a sociopsychological level, essentially become self-fulfilling prophecy.[13]

The church must—especially in terms of our war with the Left—liberate ourselves from the chains of defeatist eschatologies and narratives. In this regard it is vital for us to re-orientate ourselves in terms of the past, the present and the future, as well as the interplay between the three. It is often said that it is impossible to understand the present or envisage the future without understanding the past, but I would go even further: it is in, fact, impossible to understand the past or the present without understanding the future. Once we understand that the world will continue to improve as Christ "must reign till He has put all enemies under his feet" (I Corinthians 15:25), we will not be afraid of the future and retreat from the world, but confidently engage culture to the glory of God. One of the major problems I have with most church historians, for example, is their reference to the

---

13. D.K Matthews, *A Theology of the Cross and Kingdom: Theologia Crucis after the Reformation, Modernity and Ultramodern Tribalistic Syncretism* (Eugene, OR: Pickwick, 2019), 142.

first four centuries after the apostles as the time of the "early church." There is an inherent problem caused by this, because of the narrative implications thereof upon both our view of history and our eschatology: it ultimately sanctions an amillennial and even premillennial narrative in which the end of the world and defeat of the church is seen as impending. But it is not the unrighteous, but ultimately the righteous who will inherit the earth (Psalm 37:29). We must therefore actively forsake such false and destructive narratives in order to overcome the pacifism plaguing the church today.

We must orientate ourselves towards the future and actively work towards expanding and advancing the kingdom of Christ on earth, knowing that, even if we may not see all the fruits of our labors in our own lifetimes, our descendants generations from now most certainly will. Therefore, it is also vital not to separate or isolate our battle against the Left from the overarching battle between Christ and the forces of darkness which characterizes all of history. Because history culminates in the victory of Christ and not the antichrist, we can and should confidently engage in all socio-political, cultural and economic endeavors with the distinct purpose of cultivating every sphere of life with the knowledge that we are participating in a victory that is set, certain, and inevitable. Thus, even if our enemies may seem many, even if their power and control may seem overwhelming, even if they may seem undefeatable, we must be steadfast and remain true to our duty as soldiers of Christ's Kingdom to cast down "every high thing that exalts itself against the knowledge of God" (II Corinthians 10:5). We must never surrender the material realm to Satan and the enemies of Christ. Christ has already conquered Satan, sin, and death by means of his resurrection. Despite temporary setbacks, the world will continue to resemble His kingdom more and more as history progresses.

Because of all the very real challenges we face today, many conservative Christians are tempted by romantic idealizations of the past. We see the most degenerate contemporary practices such as Drag Queen Story Hour, remember that we didn't have this a few years back and then conclude that things are inevitably going to continue getting worse. But this is an oversimplification of reality. There were many societies in history that were as degenerate if not more degenerate than our own. Scripture also expressly condemns an idealization of the past at the cost of a future-orientated perspective: Ecclesiastes 7:10 reads "Do not say, 'Why were the former days better than these?' For you do not inquire wisely concerning this."

While not denying the dire state of Christianity today because of the infiltration of the church by Cultural Marxists, we should also not forget the gains silently being made. I recently had an online meeting with a Croatian friend in which he informed me that within the space of a few months, he had, by means of social media, come to learn about and know fellow Reformed Theonomists in both neighboring Hungary and Serbia. Just a few months prior he had thought that he may be the only person with his beliefs in that part of Europe, and now he is networking and meeting with other like-minded individuals.

The impact of the mainstream media and entertainment industry is currently also waning dramatically. Virtually no one trusts mainstream news outlets such as CNN anymore, and with good reason. The ratings and viewership figures of woke sports leagues are likewise in a freefall.[14] These encouraging developments of course provide us with ample opportunities to re-engage in these spheres of life by establishing viable, Christian alternatives.

We must also take heart in the fact that our enemies, for the most part, genuinely lack any vision for the future. Most unbelievers nowadays simply strive to maximize indulging in the great-

---

14. For example, think of the backlash the Australian Open tennis tournament and the tyrannical Australian government faced when they unjustly persecuted Novak Djokovic, the Serbian Orthodox tennis star and arguably the greatest player of all time, at the start of 2022. While Leftists justified their claim that the right decision was made to revoke his visa on the grounds that "rules should equally apply to everyone," the great irony was that the very judges who made said decision were themselves legally exempt from the tyrannical mandate on which it was based (Judicial College of Victoria, *Coronavirus and the Courts* (8 October 2021), https://www.judicial-college.vic.edu.au/resources/coronavirus-and-courts).

est material pleasures this life has to offer. But this is suicidal hedonism in which having children is seen as inconvenient and an unnecessary burden. Whether by means of birth control or by means of abortion, the Left is ultimately on the path to destroying itself in the long run. But their destruction will not be accomplished with us sitting back and doing nothing. God created us and placed us in this specific time and place for a distinct purpose, and therefore rendering God-fearing children and ensuring their perseverance in the faith by actively countering the destructive impact of Leftist propaganda through the media, schools, entertainment industry and their peers is absolutely essential to guaranteeing that your family continues to play an important role in the continuing establishment of Christ's Kingdom here on earth.

While it is true that the progress to be made by the gospel throughout the world will not simply be linear and unbroken and while there will still be challenges and dark times in our future, we can always maintain confidence in the fact that the promise of John 12:47, where Jesus proclaimed that came "to save the world," will be fulfilled in future in terms of all its cosmic significance.

CONCLUSION

The militant resistance against Marxist subversion now required of us will be a long and hard journey. While there will be some heroics along the way, most of it will entail getting our hands dirty and working hard to exercise dominion and take every square inch of creation captive in obedience to Christ. At the end of the day, we know that our King's victory is sure and that it is merely our duty to play our role and fight for His kingdom wherever our outpost may be. But we are not helpless. Believing that you are helpless is a denial of the true power of the Holy Spirit working in your life as a Christian. The sanctification of all creation starts with the battle of every individual Christian against his own sinfulness. Get your own life in order by conquering your own disobedience to God's Law. Cultivate a ruthless hatred of sin. Reform your family life. Even by doing little things in our local communities or counties, we are laying the groundwork for great divine interventions in future. Rousas John Rushdoony reminds us to hold firm to the infallible promises of Scripture even in times when the battle seems lost:

[T]he prophecies of Isaiah and of all of Scripture shall be fulfilled. Scripture is not divided; it is not made irrelevant to history. There shall be, as Genesis 3:15, Romans 16:20, and Revelation 12:9, 11 declare, victory over Satan... The postmillennial view, while seeing rises and falls in history, sees it moving to the triumph of the people of Christ, the church triumphant from pole to pole, the government of the whole world by the law of God, and then, after a long and glorious reign of peace, the Second Coming and the end of the world.[1]

We can never give up. We can never stop fighting. We must envisage the glorious future of Christendom which we have been called to help bring about by our socio-political engagement. Most importantly, we can never stop fighting *to win*. The pessimistic, defeatist, impotent, and weak Christianity prevalent in the Christian church throughout the world today is an abomination. It is the religion of losers and cowards. The expectation that the Antichrist will triumph in history entails surrendering the material world to Satan. It is an affront to God, to our risen Lord Jesus Christ, who by virtue of His resurrection has already guaranteed and sealed his own victory. It is a denial of God's sovereignty over all of creation and His promises to His people. Christ reigns and

1. Rushdoony, *Postmillennialism*, 14-15.

His kingdom will continue to advance and progress as human history unfolds. The glory days of Christendom is not behind us. It is in the future. As Psalm 22:27-29 prophecies:

> All the ends of the world shall remember and turn to the Lord, and all the families of the nations shall worship before You. For the kingdom is the Lord's, and He rules over the nations. All the prosperous of the earth shall eat and worship; All those who go down to the dust shall bow before Him.

The covenantal paradigm inherent to God's design of the world also necessitates an optimistic eschatology. Texts such as Deuteronomy 7:12-15 and Deuteronomy 28, in explaining that God punishes disobedience and blesses obedience to His commands, reveal to us an inescapable providential framework, which testifies to the fact that God has designed reality in such a way that sin, that is, disobedience to His Law always has detrimental consequences, while obedience is accompanied by blessings from His Fatherly hand. Experience confirms this. Drinking too much leads to hangovers, sexual licentiousness leads to disease and unwanted pregnancies, spending more money than you earn causes you to acquire debt, open border immigration policies lead to socio-demographic disasters, and the materialist and feminist worldview with its aversion to children leads to national and cultural suicide. Because the detrimental consequences of sin are inescapable, all societies that live in disobedience to God are doomed to either collapse or repent. There are no other alternatives. In reality, there is nothing progressive about Liberalism or Marxism. Because of the rebellion of these ideologies against the inescapable sovereignty of God, they are doomed to fail.

Even despite all the inroads made by Leftists and Marxists in systematically infiltrating and subverting our institutions—our government at all levels, our media, our schools, our universities, our social clubs—we have reason for optimism even now. As noted earlier in this book, one of the great upsides of the twenty-first century, and in all likelihood all centuries to come, is the immense reach and influence we have by virtue of the technological advances which have been made. Never in the history of the world have so many people been exposed to the truths of the gospel of Jesus Christ as they are today by virtue of the internet. The influence of the mainstream media is declining as public trust in the current establishment declines. The influence and reach of social media and alternative platforms on which Right-wing Christians are particularly active have increased tremendously over the past few years and continue to increase today. Even as censorship on traditional platforms increases, alternatives are starting to arise.

More people than ever around the Western world are now arming themselves and organizing themselves to defend their families and communities against the threats of domestic terrorism and government tyranny. Alternative currencies liberated from the control of central banks are becoming more and more popular. Even the elucidation of many orthodox theological principles in our day and age is unprecedented. Because we stand on the shoulders of giants, and perhaps also because of the unique challenges before us, we are continually able to produce a more coherent and thorough theology, especially in terms of its application to all the various dynamics of contemporary life. By merely publishing a blog post we are able to now potentially reach thousands of people with life-changing theological truths in a very short period of time. This book is only one example of an ever-growing body of solid Christian literature being published today.

Also, while we have now largely forfeited our political power in most Western countries, we often—and to our own detriment—tend to forget that civil government is only one of a number of spheres of government instituted by God. As long as Christian fathers can execute godly authority as heads of their households, we must use this to glorify God. For as long as faithful Christian men hold offices in the church, we must use that authority to advance the Kingdom. Only once we have established a culture wherein men execute these governmental offices in accordance with divine law and design can we proceed to exercising dominion over the civil sphere.

Let our hope in Christ always remain steadfast and unfailing. But at the same time, let us not deny the challenge posed by and the gravity of our current predicament. The institutional church has been greatly corrupted and is certainly not living up to the calling and royal status of the bride of Christ: the contemporary church is weak, impotent, and passive. Innumerable heretics and cowards man her pulpits. Historic Christendom already has been largely destroyed. We are most certainly on the backfoot and most of us are in the position where we have to do those dirty jobs needed to rebuild Christendom from scratch. It may entail frustrating little battles such as family conflicts about which programs to watch and not to watch on television, or it may mean going the extra mile and spending a little additional money in order to avoid supporting businesses who make their hatred of Christ and Christianity openly known.

We must remain vigilant, courageous, and steadfast in our fight to restore Christendom, even if our enemies have already declared victory and the current international global order does, humanly speaking, seem invincible. Scripture is clear that cowards who fear God's enemies more than they fear Him will not inherit the Kingdom of God (Revelation 21:8). Even in the face of the greatest trials and in the face of a seemingly invincible opposition, cowardice and despair are grave sins. It is also based on the false conception that Satan is the Lord of this world. Scripture is clear that the Holy Spirit who lives in us as greater and mightier than any force the opposition may ever bring about (1 John 4:4).

One of the most lamentable traditional translations of any biblical passage is the common translation of the Greek words θεὸς τοῦ αἰῶνος (2 Cor. 4:4), referring to Satan, as "God of this world." The Greek word for world or creation is κόσμος (*kosmos*). On the contrary, the Greek word used by Paul, αἰώνιον (*ainon*, genetive *ainos*) refers to a time period or era. In this passage, the apostle was therefore making an observation regarding the Greco-Roman culture of his time, not making an ontological claim. In other words, Paul was saying that Satan was glorified by the culture at the time as a god, not that he is indeed lord over the world in any real sense.

Another passage often invoked and abused to justify a retreat from this world is John 18:36, where Jesus answers the question of Pontius Pilate whether He is the king of the Jews by replying, "My kingdom is not of this world. If My kingdom were of this world, My servants would fight, so that I should not be delivered to the Jews; but now My kingdom is not from here." Misrepresenting these words as implying that Christ's Kingdom is strictly spiritual or otherworldly amounts to a gross ignorance regarding the context of the discussion in which Christ uttered them. It must not be overlooked that Christ was answering a question, namely whether He is King of the Jews, the very same people who were, at the time, delivering Him to Pilate to be crucified. That is why He immediately thereafter answers that His kingdom stands in opposition to the godless people who were, at that very moment, opposing his reign and wanting to kill Him (John 18:36b). When Jesus was therefore claiming that His kingdom was not "of this world," He was evidently using it in the same sense that He had used these very words, ἐκ τοῦ κόσμου, in the preceding chapter, when He said that the world hates Him and his disciples because they are not "of the world" (John 17:14). In light of this, I propose that a better translation of Jesus' words would be "not of *the* world" as opposed to "not of *this* world," as He was referring to the unregenerate status of the vast majority of people who had rejected Him at the time rather than making a claim about the nature of His kingdom. Furthermore, that this is how Jesus' words are to be understood is evident when we apply the hermeneutical principle of *analogia fidei*, that is that Scripture is to be clarified by the Holy Spirit through Scripture itself: apart from the fact that Jesus, after having conquered sin, death and evil by His resurrection, noted that all authority on earth belongs to Him alone (Matthew 28:18), Revelation 11:15 also expressly proclaims that well before the culmination of world history in the Second Coming of Christ the "kingdoms of *the world* (τοῦ κόσμου) have become the kingdoms of our Lord and of His Christ, and He will reign forever and ever!" While

Jesus sacrificed Himself to reconcile us to God, He purposefully did so to ascend to the throne of universal power and dominion. From this position He proclaims that all men are to submit to Him—or die. All men are to bend the knee to the risen and exalted Christ, whom the Father has tasked with universal judgment.

It is the risen and exalted Christ, the Conqueror of evil, sin, and death—and not Satan—who actively and sovereignly reigns over this world (Matthew 28:18; 1 Corinthians 15:25). The fact that Christ physically and bodily rose from the dead entails His Lordship over not only all spiritual but also over all physical realities and every aspect of life in the cosmos. As sovereign Lord He is actively and continually, by the power of the Holy Spirit, subduing all of His enemies. We who are part of His kingdom and enlisted in His army can therefore never cease working and fighting. We should be continually encouraged and motivated by the knowledge that His true Church, that invisible union of all His elect children from every nation, is constantly growing—even as you are reading this. Christ has positioned His church at the gates of hell for the purpose of besieging and conquering it. And this church, this currently sleeping giant, will one day arise to ruthlessly fight and conquer the haters and enemies of Christ, for whom that day will be the most unpleasant one they will have ever experienced. In the name of our conquering King, we will make sure of that.

Everyone is dull-hearted, without knowledge;
Every metalsmith is put to shame by the
carved image;
For his molded image is falsehood,
And there is no breath in them.
They are futile, a work of errors;
In the time of their punishment they
shall perish.
The Portion of Jacob is not like them,
For He is the Maker of all things;
And Israel is the tribe of His inheritance.
The Lord of hosts is His name.
You are My battle-ax and weapons of war:
For with you I will break the nation in pieces;
With you I will destroy kingdoms;
With you I will break in pieces the horse and
its rider;
With you I will break in pieces the chariot and
its rider;
With you also I will break in pieces man
and woman;
With you I will break in pieces old and young;
With you I will break in pieces the young man
and the maiden;
With you also I will break in pieces the shep-
herd and his flock;
With you I will break in pieces the farmer and
his yoke of oxen;
And with you I will break in pieces governors
and rulers.

–Jeremiah 51:17-23

ABOUT THE AUTHOR

Dr. Jan Adriaan Schlebusch (born 1989) is a historian, philosopher, and theologian from South Africa. He holds two BA degrees (Theology and Latin) and a Master's degree in Philosophy from the University of the Free State. In 2018, he graduated with a PhD from the Faculty of Theology and Religious Studies at the University of Groningen in the Netherlands. He is the executive director and a senior researcher at the Pactum Institute, an independent academic research institute dedicated to the scholarly advancement of biblical Christianity in the fields of theology and the humanities. Other works by Dr. Schlebusch include:

Cartesianism and Reformed Scholastic Theology: A Comparative Study of the Controversy between Christoph Wittich and Petrus van Mastricht, M.A. thesis, University of the Free State, 2013.

Strategic Narratives: Groen van Prinsterer as Nineteenth-Century Statesman-Historian, PhD diss., University of Groningen, 2018.

"Decentering the Status Quo: The Rhetorically-Sanctioned Political Engagement of Groen van Prinsterer," *Trajecta. Religion, Culture and Society in the Low Countries* 29(2), 2020: 141-159.

"Democrat or Traditionalist? The Epistemology behind Groen van Prinsterer's Notion of Political Authority," *Journal for Christian Scholarship* 56(3-4), 2020: 113-129.

"The Role of Familialism in Counter-Enlightenment Social Ontology," *Journal for Christian Scholarship* 57(3-4), 2021: 135-147.